FROM RAFT TO RAFT

FROM RAFT TO RAFT

An Incredible Voyage from Tahiti to Chile and Back

By BENGT DANIELSSON

From the narrative of ALAIN BRUN

Translated from the Swedish by F. H. LYON

Skyhorse Publishing

Published by arrangement with Doubleday, an imprint of The Knopf Doubleday Publishing Group, a division of Random House, Inc.

Visit our website at www.skyhorsepublishing.com.

10 9 8 7 6 5 4 3 2 1

Library of Congress Cataloging-in-Publication Data is available on file.

ISBN: 978-1-62087-782-1

Printed in the United States of America

CONTENTS

Introduction

AN IMMORTAL SEA ROVER

It was early one morning at the end of October 1956. While most of my fellow-passengers on board the French Pacific Line's ten thousand-tonner *Tahitien* were still asleep, I hurried up on deck to get the earliest possible sight of the most beautiful island in the world, Tahiti, to which I was now returning for the fifth time. It was still pitch dark, and it was a long time before I could distinguish with difficulty a jagged silhouette to starboard. Were we already so near my longed-for goal? My uncertainty was soon removed, for only a quarter of an hour later the first faint light of dawn revealed that it was the neighbouring island of Moorea I had seen. At the same time, and just as suddenly, the central peaks of Tahiti, more than 7000 feet high, stood out clearly against the quickly lightening sky thirteen miles farther east. The mountains, cleft by erosion, with their many ridges and valleys, were at first as grey and lifeless as a moon landscape, but the nearer we came and the higher the sun rose into the sky, the greener, softer and richer in changing colours they became.

Astonished and delighted to find that the picture I had preserved in my heart during my two years' absence had been so faithful a copy of reality, I let my eyes travel round the scene I had known so well, from the historic Matavai Bay to eastward to the bare Cape Tataa in the west, whence, according to an old Tahitian tradition, the souls of the dead dived down into the sea to return to Havaiki, the Polynesians' legendary fatherland and paradise. Although the whole population were converted and had been regular churchgoers for more than a hundred years, during my earlier stays in the island I had actually met now and then a wrinkled old man or woman who still believed in this simple transmigration theory. As I slowly went back to my cabin to pack, I wondered how many of these old people I should find still alive.

When I returned to my look-out post on the upper promenade deck about an hour later, with the rest of the family, we were already at the opening in the coral reef off the little capital Papeete, whose ungainly concrete buildings and sun-bleached plank houses, mercifully enough, were almost concealed by the flowering flame, or royal poinciana, trees along the water-front. Everywhere I saw well-known landmarks which summoned up pleasant and amusing recollections. With the pilot in charge, the ship glided swiftly in through the narrow entrance, and now we could even make out the names of the white copra schooners which were moored at the quay.

Suddenly I started. What on earth was that queer craft lying there right in front of the Post Office, in just the same place where our one and only *Kon-Tiki* raft had found sanctuary nine years before? For a few seconds I almost thought that time had stood still and that it really was our balsa raft which lay there, but a friendly 'bonjour' from the harbour-master, who had just come aboard, quickly brought me back to reality. When I looked more closely I saw too that the raft at the quay differed from ours in several respects, most notably in being built of bamboo and having two double masts. Bursting with curiosity, I asked my friend the harbour-master whence this new raft came. He gave me a searching look and replied:

'She doesn't come from anywhere, for she was built here. Are you pulling my leg, or do you really mean to say that you have not yet heard of Eric de Bisschop's new expedition? He's going to sail to Chile in that tub—*Tahiti Nui* he calls her—at the beginning of next month, with four other lunatics. Here in Tahiti people have been talking of nothing else for months past.'

A few minutes later we were at the quay, and our conversation was interrupted by a party of noisy friends, who embraced us in the Tahitian manner and hung such masses of wreaths round our necks that we were almost stifled by the strong scent of the flowers. At least as many more friends were waiting for us on the quay. When at last we had done with all the customs and passport formalities and got into the waiting taxi, we were almost buried under wreaths. So I only got a hasty glimpse of the shining yellow bamboo raft as we drove past her along the quay, but that was enough to set my imagination working.

'Queer, your not realizing at once that that was your friend Eric's raft,' my wife Marie-Thérèse said with a teasing smile as we rolled along between the palm groves which began immediately outside the town.

She was right. I ought to have realized immediately that the only person in Tahiti who could have thought of anything of the kind was that incurable sea rover Eric de Bisschop. I use the words sea rover because they are undeniably the most suitable, but I hope that they will not suggest anything like dirtiness, vulgarity and poverty, for in appearance, manners and birth Eric was a real aristocrat and, despite his Flemish name, came of a genuine French family of title. He himself never used the title of Baron he had inherited from his father, but on the few occasions when I heard anyone else do so I could not help thinking of another famous Baron, von Munchhausen, for like him Eric used to tell the most incredible stories—though his stories, unlike those of the German, were all true. Another but less important difference was that all Eric's strange adventures had been at sea. Eric loved the sea with the same unreasoning, passionate love which other men have for particularly attractive women. Unfortunately his love was unreturned, for most of his many voyages had ended in disaster—from which, however, he had in some way or another always managed to escape alive. Altogether he had been saved from a premature and apparently certain death in the billows no less than six times, which must be a world record in its way.

When Eric's violent passion for the sea first made itself noticeable in his teens, his worried parents tried to canalize it as best they could by having him trained as a hydrographer, knowing that most able hydrographers finished up as departmental chiefs in the head office of the hydrographic service. But, as Eric had feared, his duties were very much of a routine nature, and when the first world war broke out he was glad to leave them and take command of a minesweeper. But he had not been at sea in the English Channel for many days when a German submarine sank his vessel. Eric, who could not swim, was fished out of the water in the nick of time by a French patrol boat. After this the service became so uneventful and monotonous that he promptly exchanged it for the newly created air arm. But he did not thereby lose contact with the sea: on the contrary one might—at the risk of being taken to task for cheap humour—say that this was intensified, for while on reconnaissance over the Mediterranean some time later, his engine stopped unaccountably and he fell from a height of some 2500 feet. The pilot of another flying boat managed to get down to sea level and keep the unconscious Eric afloat till a rescue boat arrived. The rest of the war he spent in hospital.

During the enforced period of rest that followed Eric fell in love, got married, took over a timber business and for several years lived an almost normal citizen's life. But by degrees his longing for the sea got the better of him: he bought a three-master, in which he began to carry timber between West Africa and France. One stormy day the cargo shifted, and before the crew could shorten sail the ship capsized and sank. Eric and a few of his men were picked up by another vessel, which by a stroke of luck happened to be passing the scene of the disaster at the right moment. Simultaneously with the loss of his beloved three-master his marriage was shipwrecked. The reason was simply that his intractable need of liberty made him unsuited to the married state. Consequently his first wife was no more able to keep him than any other of the many women in his life.

In better spirits than for a long time he spent the last money in his pocket on a steamer passage to China. He himself declares in one of his frank and charming books that it was the 'mysteries of the Pacific' that drew him so far afield. At the same time he sought for 'something which could entirely fill his life and make it worth living'. This was of course an extremely vague programme, more natural in a teenager than in a man of thirty-seven. Eric, however, sensibly enough began his new life by joining the police force in the French Concession in Shanghai, which gave him an opportunity both of forming rather more concrete plans and of earning enough money to carry them out.

A few years later—to be exact, at the end of 1932—his plans had crystallized and he was ready to start on a cruise in the South Seas to study the ocean currents. His vessel was a junk of forty tons, *Fou Po,* designed by himself, and his companion was a colleague from the police force ten years younger than himself: Tatibouet was his name, but Eric always called him Tati. Hardly had they left Shanghai when a fearful cyclone came sweeping down from the north and gave *Fou Po* an unwelcome free ride which did not end till she fetched up five days later on the rocky northern coast of Formosa. A band of slant-eyed men made their way out to the wreck and rescued the half-drowned partners in misfortune. Next day, when they had more or less recovered and returned to the scene of the wreck, they found to their consternation that their noble rescuers had also taken care to strip the vessel of all loose and detachable objects.

Any other man would certainly have given up all plans for a long voyage after such a catastrophe, but Eric possessed two qualities, obstinacy (not to say pig-headedness) and charm, which came to his help now as they had done so often before and were to do so many times in the future. Only a few months after his return to China he had persuaded a well-disposed French consul to present him with the necessary timber, and with Tati and a few Chinese workmen he completed a new junk, which he naturally christened *Fou Po II*. Compared with her predecessor's forty tons, the new junk was of only twelve tons, a more suitable size for a crew of two—or perhaps I ought to say a captain and a crew of one, for Eric was and always remained the obvious and natural leader. To make his now very slender funds last a little longer, Eric had what seemed to him the brilliant idea of investing the greater part of them in a stock of Chinese antiquities, convinced that he could sell these at a good profit in foreign ports.

Fou Po II exceeded all Eric's and Tati's expectations, and no cyclones appeared. They reached Mindanao, the most southerly of the Philippine Islands, without mishap, and set out thence across the Pacific to begin their studies with a close investigation of the strong counter-current which according to the charts flows right across the Pacific from west to east in this latitude in exactly the opposite direction to the trade winds. One of the most important anthropological articles of faith at this time was that the Polynesians had used this route on their long voyage by canoe from their primeval home somewhere in Asia to the distant South Sea islands. But no anthropologist or oceanographer had studied the equatorial counter-current, as this important ocean current was called, at all thoroughly, and the little that was known of it was based on casual and scattered observations. In his enthusiasm Eric decided to follow it for its whole length all the way to the Galapagos Islands, about 9000 miles, a distance corresponding to about a third of the world's circumference.

It was as important to ascertain the breadth of the current as its direction and strength, and therefore, instead of setting his course due east for the distant Galapagos Islands, Eric began to make long tacks. By this method, of course, not such rapid progress was made, and a month later *Fou Po II* was only 600 sea miles nearer her destination, which at this rate it would take more than a year to reach. This did not cause Eric's enthusiasm to flag in any way, but as time passed Tati became more and more dissatisfied and gloomy. Eric lent only an absent ear to the lamentations of his crew and placidly continued his zigzag course, becoming more and more convinced that the equatorial current was too weak, and the wind blowing the opposite way too strong, for the Polynesians ever to have been able to make use of it during their migrations. Eric's interest in Polynesian navigation and anthropology, which finally became his dominating interest, dates from this time.

If Tati had been the only passenger on board Eric would certainly have continued to pay no attention to his opinions, for where a discovery was to be made, or a theory proved correct, he was always ruthless. But about this time he found that masses of unwelcome stowaways were also on board—namely a whole colony of ship-worms, which had bored their way into the planks below the water-line. Eric, therefore, at last broke off his studies and turned back to have the hull repaired and sheathed with copper plates at some convenient shipyard in what was then the Dutch East Indies. After a short search he found a yard at Ceram in Amboina, where some clever natives did the work well and quickly. This unexpected outlay, however, made such a big hole in his funds that he at once decided to make a trip to Sydney in order to sell some of his Chinese antiques.

Instead of taking the shortest route through the Torres Strait, Eric chose to sail right round Australia from the western side—a more sensible decision than it seems, for strong following winds should normally have helped them to make a quick and easy passage. Unfortunately the winds did not behave at all as they should, according to the charts and the nautical manuals, and instead of helpful favourable winds the unlucky pair met with such violent gales that their junk was reduced to a wreck. By superhuman efforts they at last succeeded, more dead than alive, in getting ashore at the little pearl fishing village of Broome, on the north-west coast of Australia.

As they still wanted to get to Sydney they decided to make their way through the Torres Strait, shallow and full of reefs. Unfortunately *Fou Po II* lacked something which most of the boats which venture into those waters have; namely, a motor. All Eric's skill and Tati's sharp eyes did not prevent them from running aground again and again, and finally they were dismasted just before they slid out into the open water of the Gulf of Papua on the other side of the Strait. Their beloved junk drifted helplessly into the mouth of a river on the south coast of New Guinea and stuck fast in the deep mud of the bank amid a tangle of uprooted trees, broken-off branches and other debris. While they were trying to get their bearings, a party of naked savages with nose-pins and sharp-pointed spears emerged from the belt of mangroves and gazed at them hungrily. This gave Eric and Tati an unpleasant reminder that most of the natives of New Guinea were still cannibals. They were firmly convinced that the savages would soon return with the head cook of the tribe and a large cooking pot, but when after a long time they did reappear they had with them a couple of neatly dressed missionaries and a long rope.

When the two valiant partners at last continued their voyage at the beginning of 1935, after an exceedingly pleasant time with both converted and unconverted cannibals, Eric decided that they could just as well wait till they got to California (!) to sell their Chinese antiques, and despite Tati's protests steered up towards the Equator to resume, in passing, his interesting studies of the current. Except that Eric was so weakened by malaria, which he had contracted in New Guinea, that he fell into the water during a visit to the Solomon Islands and would certainly have been drowned if the faithful Tati had not jumped in after him, all went well. After two months of zigzagging Tati, quite understandably, was again sick to death of the equatorial counter-current and obstinately demanded to be put ashore at once. Eric saw at last that he must give way to his crew of one if it was not to mutiny.

The nearest land was the Marshall Islands—one of which, Bikini, later became world-famous—but Eric was not particularly keen on landing there, for the Marshall Islands, like all the other Micronesian islands, had been Japanese mandated territory since the end of the first world war, and the Japanese had always brusquely turned away all foreign visitors. Tati, however, had now a fixed idea, to get ashore, and he would not listen to reason. Eric, therefore, landed on the nearest atoll, Jaluit, with unpleasant anticipations. These were justified, for the Japanese commandant immediately subjected the unexpected vistors to a third degree cross-examination which he assured them would not end till they had confessed that they were American spies. But when a fortnight had passed, and Eric and Tati had still not made the desired confession, the commandant suddenly lost patience: without a word of apology he sent them on board the junk again and roughly ordered them to leave the Marshall Islands as quickly as possible. They took him at his word and immediately hoisted all the sail the rigging would carry.

Eric, who now seems at last to have realized that Tati was not as much interested in ocean currents as he was, announced curtly that he meant to put him ashore at Hawaii: the fact that this meant a little detour of 4,000 miles did not trouble him at all. Only a few days later they began to notice a nauseous fetid smell. It seemed to come from their store-room, and when they opened the door they saw at once what had happened. Some of the commandant's minions had evidently searched the boat while they were being interrogated and, presumably hoping to find some compromising documents or miniature infernal machines, had gone to the length of opening all their tins of preserves and carefully soldered boxes of provisions. The water tank they had mercifully left untouched and almost full. When Eric and Tati had thrown overboard all the food that had gone bad, all they had left was a packet of ship's biscuits.

For three weeks they lived on biscuits, water and a soup made of grease. At first, of course, they tried to fish, but all their attempts were without result because they had no proper bait. So in order not to waste their quickly diminishing strength, henceforward they concentrated their energies on reaching their far-off destination as quickly as possible. The currents and winds were unfavourable, and life on board became one long nightmare. From the beginning of the fourth week they were so exhausted that they could not even keep a course, but began to drift. Towards the end of the fifth week they at last sighted land, a misty vision of a high, bare, rocky coast. They tried to sit up, but the effort was too great and they fainted away. When they recovered consciousness they were surroundeed by the most repulsive, horrible collection of monstrosities they had ever seen. They both thought at first that they had been transported to a well-known burning hot place underground, but one of their rescuers explained matters. They had drifted ashore in the middle of the leper colony of Kalaupapa, on the north side of Molokai in the Hawaii group. Their joy at having come through alive yet again was swiftly dissipated when they learnt that their dear *Fou Po II* had been smashed against the rocks and that all their log-books, notes and other belongings had been lost.

During their long stay in hospital Eric read numbers of anthropological books. A picture of a Polynesian double canoe gave him an idea. Why not continue his interrupted study of the ocean currents on board such a craft as this, well-tested and sea-worthy? He would thus be able to study Polynesian navigation at the same time. He was still firmly decided to make all his future voyages alone. But what would become of poor Tati? To return to France by steamer would be very expensive, and Tati had long given Eric all the money he had. Eric generously offered first to make a trip to France with Tati, just as if it had been a little cruise along the coast and not a daring journey halfway round the globe. It was an absurdly magnificent gesture, but Tati, who by this time had adopted Eric's grandiose ideas of life, quietly accepted the offer. The two inseparable friends, both equally happy at the prospect of being separated at last, immediately set about building a boat for the third time.

The queer vessel was completed a year later, and at the beginning of March 1937 Eric and Tati took a glad farewell of Hawaii and a crowd of newly acquired friends who, until the last minute, persisted in calling their modest double canoe, only thirty-seven feet long, 'the two coffins'. They themselves had named her *Kaimiloa,* after a famous canoe in a Hawaiian legend. *Kaimiloa* quickly showed herself to be not only a steady and easily managed craft, but also a notably fast sailer. Delighted that his new creation had proved such an excellent seaboat, and eager to keep his promise to Tati, Eric hoisted all sail and carried out with extraordinary precision and elegance one of the longest and quickest voyages which have ever been undertaken in a craft of this size. The first 2300 miles, from Hawaii to the Wallis Islands, were covered in a little over a month without calling anywhere. Thence Eric resolutely set a course for the Torres Strait, which he passed through this time with such certainty that it almost looked as if he remembered the exact position of every reef from his earlier passage in *Fou Po II.*

The rest of the voyage as far as Bali went easily and quickly, and all earlier records were beaten.

But the voyage across the Indian Ocean was even more striking. With the kindly help of an unusually strong north-east monsoon, *Kaimiloa* rushed along like a racing yacht and arrived at Cape Town a mere fifty-nine days later. Her average speed had been not less than 100 miles a day, which is unique for so long a voyage. Perhaps it should be added that Eric and Tati would certainly have made the crossing still more quickly if they had not run into a storm just south of the Cape of Good Hope which smashed *Kaimiloa*'s rudder and drove them down to the edge of the polar ice. The next stage, from Cape Town to Tangier, took as much as 100 days, but they went out of their way to visit the Azores and Portugal, though curiously enough they did not land at either.

Tati, delighted to be at home at last and firmly resolved never to undertake any more long voyages under sail, took a hurried farewell of his captain as soon as they reached their final destination, Cannes, and disappeared. But Eric was still as fascinated as ever by the mysteries of the Pacific, and did not mean to stay any longer in France than was absolutely necessary. The *Kaimiloa* was an extraordinarily good boat, there were no two opinions about that: but that did not mean that she could not be improved, Eric thought. But the improvements he wanted to make, however, were unusually numerous, and it ended in his building quite a new boat with two outriggers, which most suitably received a double name, *Kaimiloa-Wakea*. Just before this a charming and determined American girl with the pretty Hawaiian name Papaleaiaina, whom he had met in Honolulu, had arrived. Instead of the solitary cruise which he had originally intended, he hastily and gaily decided on a honeymoon voyage to the South Seas with Papaleaiaina. The newly married couple left France in May 1940, just before the fall of France.

Kaimiloa-Wakea was both faster and safer than her predecessor, and Eric's navigation was as fine as ever. But through a stroke of ill-luck, such as he encountered all his life with hideous regularity, soon after she had sailed, one dark night near the Canary Islands, *Kaimiloa-Wakea* found herself in some mysterious manner under the bows of a Spanish fishing boat. The beautiful canoe was cut in two and sank in a few minutes. Eric still could not swim, but Papaleaiaina could, and she managed to keep him from sinking till the Spaniards could launch a boat and pick them up.

This new escape from drowning was followed by one of the most fantastic episodes in Eric's adventurous life. He and his young wife were fearfully unhappy in France, to which they had been able to return only with great difficulty after a long time of waiting in the Canary Islands, and he wanted to resume his South Seas studies at all costs. But how could he do this without boat or money, and in the middle of the war? Eric solved this apparently insoluble problem with admirable ingenuity by getting himself appointed French consul in Honolulu as soon as the United States entered into diplomatic relations with the Vichy Government. Seen in the light of subsequent events, his action seems purely opportunist and foolish. But to judge this episode rightly it should be known that Eric, in accordance with old family tradition, was a Royalist, and that his parents had long been neighbours and friends of Marshal Pétain. Eric therefore regarded Pétain's personal rule as a step in the right direction, i.e., towards the restoration of the monarchy, and on account of his personal ties of friendship with the old Marshal relied on him even more blindly than the rest of his countrymen, who at that time—it must not be forgotten—with extremely few exceptions still regarded Pétain as the saviour of France.

People in Honolulu liked Eric very much, and he became very popular, but when the Vichy Government began to lose its independence and prestige, his position as consul became increasingly difficult. Eventually a point was reached at which the authorities suspected him of being a Japanese spy and put him under arrest. This time, however, the results were less disastrous than ten years before, when the Japanese commandant of Jaluit had suspected him of being an American spy. The authorities soon saw the absurdity of the charge and released him with a half-hearted excuse. As soon as the war was over he immediately began to look about for a suitable vessel for the long-postponed South Seas cruise which he was now firmly resolved to undertake.

As he could not find a Polynesian double canoe, he finally decided for a Chinese junk of 150 tons, *Cheng Ho*. She had originally been a smart pleasure yacht, but during the war had degenerated into an officers' floating mess at Pearl Harbour. The American Navy had just restored her to her owner, who was eager to find some profitable use for her. Eric, as careless and naïve as ever in economic and practical things, and evidently convinced that business and scientific study could be combined, at once formed a company with him to buy up copra and sell foodstuffs, cloth and other goods in French Polynesia.

Eric's partner prudently remained on shore during the first voyage. When Eric at last returned to Honolulu, delighted with all the peculiar ocean currents and natives he had encountered, an examination of the accounts revealed that the cruise in some incomprehensible manner showed a loss. Eric was utterly astonished, and wanted to set out on another trip at once to make good the loss. His companion, however, cold-bloodedly started a lawsuit, which went on for weeks and weeks, and hardly had the two parties reached a settlement when a new lawsuit seemed to be impending.

This was too much for Eric, who saw his newly-won liberty threatened. He hurriedly scraped together a crew, boarded *Cheng Ho,* set a course for Tahiti, and disappeared for ever out of his partner's life and that of his wife. Ordinarily at least eight men were needed to sail the big junk, but strange to say Eric and his two inexperienced companions accomplished the long voyage of 2,400 miles without misadventure in eighteen days. This audacious performance caused a great sensation, and Eric's unlucky partner was not alone in condemning him in severe language for his (to put it mildly) rash action. The only possible excuse which can be offered in this and many similar cases was that Eric was unfortunately born a few hundred years too late and that he ought to have lived in the sixteenth or seventeenth centuries, when such generally respected professions as those of pirate and *conquistador* were open to those who found a quiet life at home irksome.

It was just after this daring escapade, which took place in 1949, that I met Eric for the first time. He was lively and, despite his age (nearly sixty), as merry as a schoolboy. I fell for his charm almost immediately. In spite of our having diametrically opposite views about almost everything we parted the best of friends. During the next two years, which I spent in the Tuamotu group, Eric turned up now and again with his comical junk, and more than once he stayed a day or two longer than was necessary solely to convince me of the correctness of his, to say the least, revolutionary anthropological theories. I had a definite impression that the copra and retail goods business was in a bad way, and I was right, for some time later the company went smash.

Eric took this reverse very calmly, not to say nonchalantly, and as usual he had a new surprise in store: he not only applied for but at once obtained a newly-created post as land surveyor in the Austral group, which consists of five mountainous islands, remote and difficult of access, 300 miles south of Tahiti. Years passed without my hearing anything from Eric or about him, except that he was writing a long and learned book on Polynesian navigation and that he was immensely popular owing to his Solomon-like way of settling quarrels between landowners. I was convinced, as everyone else was, that old age had at last made itself felt and that he had settled down to a quiet life for good and all. Now, however, after all that I had heard and seen of his raft expedition, I saw that he had only withdrawn to the Austral Islands for a few years to prepare himself for the last and greatest sea adventure of his life.

Eager to obtain rather fuller information about Eric's ambitious plans, I ignored the countless suitcases and trunks which I really ought to have been unpacking, and returned to Papeete the very next morning. I spent a considerable time shouting on the quay before Eric appeared in the doorway of the hut-like cabin, which took up the greater part of the bamboo raft's deck. His hair had grown much whiter in the two years which had passed since I last saw him, and he looked tired and worried. But when he saw me his face brightened a good deal, and he ran out a plank so that I might go on board.

As soon as I had sat down in the spacious cabin, Eric began to speak at once, as though anxious to forestall an attack from my side. He said, not without a certain bitterness in his voice:

'Imitations of your *Kon-Tiki* voyage have degenerated into a futile sport for a long time past, so I'm not surprised at everybody shaking their heads and asking of what use my expedition can be. But I can assure that I am just as serious, and have just as much of a scientific object as Thor Heyerdahl, when he decided to make his raft expedition ten years ago. The only difference is that I want to prove another theory, quite the opposite of his. But I don't know if there's any object in my going on, for you'll only laugh at my theories and certainly think me crazy . . .'

I earnestly assured him that in the first place I could be neither an opponent nor a supporter of his theories, as he had not yet told me what they were, and in the second place that I had a soft spot for madmen. Eric, visibly relieved, produced a chart of the Pacific and continued:

'As my expedition will be compared with the voyage of the *Kon-Tiki* anyway, I may as well take Thor Heyerdahl's theories as my starting point. I quite agree with him that there are many identical artifacts and customs, not to say plants, in South America and in the Polynesian islands. But when it comes to explaining these similarities we do not agree. According to Thor Heyerdahl they exist because the first immigrants into Polynesia were a fair-skinned people from Peru, who sailed across the Pacific on balsa rafts and settled in the islands about fifteen hundred years ago. I, on the contrary, after twenty years of study and reflection, have come to the conclusion that the similarities are due to the fact that Polynesian sea-dogs repeatedly made the long voyage to South America and back in prehistoric times and thus both influenced and were influenced by different Indian tribes. So what we have here, in my opinion, is not a migration from one area to another but simply cultural exchanges such as have always taken place and are still taking place between different peoples—as, for example, when American women follow Parisian dress fashions and French musicians play American jazz.'

'But that's not a new theory at all,' I unkindly remarked. 'At least a dozen anthropologists, in various books and articles, have maintained that the Polynesians, on their daring long voyages across the South Seas, reached the South American coast once or several times. My countryman Erland Nordenskiöld, for example, published a study as long ago as 1931, in which—'

'I know perfectly well what Nordenskiöld, Frederici, Dixon, Rivet, Buck, Hornell, Emory and all the rest of them have written,' Eric interrupted me in a thoroughly pugnacious tone. 'But none of them know anything about navigation, and so they move peoples here and there over the map like chessmen, without regard to the practical problems. Buck imagines, for example, that Polynesian double canoes could sail direct from Tahiti or Mangareva to South America, several thousand miles, right against the strong easterly trade wind, which blows non-stop all the year round. What is new and valuable in my theory is that I show not only what route, but also what kind of craft, the Polynesians used on their voyages to and from South America. Here, look at the map. Wherever the Polynesians who went to America started from, you can be sure that they went down to about 40 degrees south, where strong westerly winds prevail. When they got close to South America the Humboldt Current gave them a free lift up to Peru: and from there, of course, they could easily return to Polynesia with the help of the easterly trade winds and currents, as your *Kon-Tiki* expedition showed. Everyone to whom I have propounded this simple theory, however, has assured me that it is so stormy at 40 degrees south that any Polynesian crew which dared to make such a rash attempt would have been lost at once. So it is mainly to show that the southern route is the only practicable one that I am prepared to make this experiment. Of all the anthropologists who have taken an interest in Polynesian navigation, Thor Heyerdahl is the only one who has attempted anything of the kind, and therefore I have much more respect for him than for all my other opponents put together.'

I nodded reflectively, and then put a question which had long been on the tip of my tongue:

'But, Eric, why don't you make your voyage of demonstration in a double canoe instead of a bamboo raft? As far as I know outrigger canoes and double canoes were the only vessels the Polynesians had in old times.'

'You are partly right, for no European has ever seen a real seaworthy Polynesian sailing raft made of bamboo,' Eric replied. 'But to jump to the conclusion that there *never* have been any such craft in Polynesia, as everyone has done so far, is surely rather hasty. All proper models had undoubtedly disappeared at the time when the islands were discovered, for the reason, which anyone can understand, that the Polynesians had long before this ceased to make long voyages between the different groups of islands. But degenerate forms of sailing rafts were still to be found everywhere, and even today, on a few islands, some old man can be found who can describe these craft.'

I must have looked dubious, for Eric raised his voice and added, in a still more decided tone:

'Indeed, sailing rafts must have been used all over the Pacific in remote antiquity. For unless one assumes them to be derived from a common original type, how can one explain the fact that rafts of the same kind are still in use on both sides of the Pacific, in Peru in the east and in Formosa and Indo-China in the west?'

'So that is why you have fitted out your raft with Peruvian centreboards and Chinese rig at the same time?' I put in.

Eric nodded gravely. I myself found it hard to take this method of reconstructing a prehistoric type of raft really seriously. But as my intention here is primarily to give an idea of what sort of man Eric de Bisschop was and what his own purpose in undertaking his raft expedition was, I shall omit the keen discussion which followed. It was not interrupted till, an hour or two later, there was a loud knocking on the cabin door.

Eric called 'Come in!' and his new visitor entered. He was an extremely short but powerfully built man who could not have been more than twenty-five. His manner was direct and bold, and he made a very pleasant impression at once. Eric introduced him. His name was Alain Brun, and he was one of Eric's four companions. Alain wanted to know how and where the provisions, which had just arrived, were to be stowed. Eric replied with a touch of impatience that Alain was a good enough seaman to be able to decide this question himself, and continued our discussion vigorously. He had embarked upon a long, critical analysis of a new objection to this theory which I had put forward, when he was interrupted by a fresh knocking. This time it was an autograph hunter, who had forgotten both his pen and his book but wanted an autograph all the same. Almost simultaneously the three other members of the crew arrived to ask Eric's advice about some important matter. I took a hasty leave of Eric and hurried home to get on with my unpacking at last.

Eric sailed a fortnight after this conversation. His departure was the occasion for a real popular festival, of the kind which is rarely seen in Tahiti except during the annual canoe races held as part of the Fourteenth of July celebrations. All the Europeans in the island, headed by the governor, and thousands of Tahitians had made a pilgrimage to the quay. Other Tahitians had come in outrigger canoes and paddled slowly and expectantly round the flower-decked raft. Lively talk, laughter and song were heard on all sides. Suddenly a roll of drums fell on our ears. The noise ceased, and everyone looked wonderingly in the direction from which the roll of drums came. Next moment a band of Tahitian hula girls in straw skirts emerged from the scrub along the shore and swayed rhythmically forward towards Eric and his companions. When the girls had danced an exciting Tahitian *upaupa* and sung a pretty farewell song, specially composed for the occasion, they took off their wreaths of white *tiare* flowers and hung them round the necks of the delighted raftsmen. It was a typical Tahitian farewell, of the kind which in old times the population only gave to really important chiefs who were about to undertake a long and hazardous voyage.

Eric and his comrades, visibly moved, went on board *Tahiti Nui* and climbed up on to the cabin roof, while a waiting tug took the raft in tow. I followed the two ill-assorted craft with my eyes till they disappeared behind Tataa, the Cape Farewell of departing souls in the Tahitian mythology. To the last moment the five men—one slight little figure in a white vest and khaki shorts and four athletic forms in loin-cloths—stood on the roof waving cheerfully to the crowds on shore.

Two years later almost as large a crowd assembled on the quay at Papeete to welcome the raftsmen back. But this time no jesting, laughter or singing was heard, and the grave-faced hula girls who had mingled with the other spectators were all dressed in white Sunday frocks. All Tahiti had known for several days past that the raft expedition had ended disastrously and that Eric de Bisschop was dead.

The French gunboat which had been sent to fetch the survivors glided slowly in towards the quay with her flag at half-mast. While the officers and crew stood rigidly at attention, and many of the men and women on the quay sobbed aloud, a simple wooden coffin was hoisted up out of the interior of the vessel and placed on the deck of an army troop transport lorry. Not till some time after the lorry had driven away did the other members of the expedition come slowly down the gangway. They were very laconic and tight-lipped, as if they had not yet recovered from a terrible shock, and their curt phrases were soon drowned in the deafening babble which broke out around them. But the little I heard conveyed clearly that Alain Brun was the hero and that the perilous adventure would certainly have ended in a still greater tragedy if he had not kept his promise to Eric de Bisschop and accompanied him on the return voyage from Chile to Polynesia.

By a lucky chance, only a few days later Alain became my neighbour in the Paea district on the west coast of Tahiti. Our many common interests soon led us to seek one another's society more frequently. To begin with, Alain found it difficult to speak openly and freely of the painful memories which seemed unceasingly to occupy his mind. But then one evening he suddenly thawed, and slowly and circumstantially, as if making a confession to me, he at last told me in plain language what had happened during the two long years from his cheerful departure from Tahiti in November 1956 to his melancholy return in September 1958.

Here is his story in the complete form which it finally assumed when Alain had told it over again once or twice and thoroughly searched his memory. That those who have never had the advantage of meeting personally the man who became Eric de Bisschop's last intimate friend and worthy deputy as leader of the expedition, may be able to get to know him pretty well at once, I will begin at the beginning and describe the long chain of strange events which led to his first meeting with Eric.

So I call upon Alain to take up the tale.

Chapter 1

APPRENTICESHIP

It is really my brother Michel's fault more than my own that I have spent more than a year of my life on board different rafts, all of which have shown an unpleasant inclination to sink under my feet or to fall to pieces. But now, when I sit at ease in a comfortable chair in a cool palm-thatched house on the shore of a shining lagoon, and think over my experiences, I cannot feel any grievance against him. On the contrary, I am grateful to him. For without his unsought intervention I should probably never have settled down in Tahiti and should most certainly never have known that remarkable, fascinating man, Eric de Bisschop.

On closer consideration, however, I think I can claim for myself some credit for the turn my life has taken, because it was I alone who made the vital decision, immediately after the end of the last world war, to go to sea. I was only fourteen and had lost my father and mother a long time before. I had spent the years of the war in Algeria, in various children's colonies and with a series of temporary foster-parents. As soon as traffic between North Africa and France got going again I went over to Marseilles to find my brothers and sisters, from whom I had heard nothing for years.

With the exception of Michel, a year older than myself, I gradually found them all in different children's homes or with different foster-parents. My first idea was to become a baker, so as to be able at last to gorge on bread and sweet cakes after all the deprivations of the war years. But all the bakers whom I approached seemed to divine my intentions at once, for they only roared with laughter and turned me away. Instead, I entered the school of navigation at Marseilles in the hope that I might thus get a free trip to a distant country unscarred by war and still flowing with milk and honey.

Three months later my theoretical training as a seaman was finished; and to my delight I was immediately engaged as a ship's boy on board a vessel bound for Indo-China. Certainly we never got farther than Madagascar, where we were hung up for several weeks with engine trouble. But like most of those on board I did not mind at all, and spent every centime of my pay on tropical fruit and visits to restaurants. During the next three years I continued to sail between Marseilles and various African ports in old tubs which ought to have been scrapped long ago, but were kept in service on account of the desperate scarcity of tonnage. It was a hard and rough life, but at least I was sure of my board and lodging, and that was all I asked at that time.

At the beginning of 1949 I was signed on in an—even for French post-war conditions—unusually rusty and ill-kept ship which was bound for Australia and the French possessions in the Pacific. I was only moderately pleased, for it was a five months' voyage, and there were long intervals between the short calls at ports. Forty-seven days after leaving Marseilles we had got no farther than Tahiti, at that time only a name on the map to me. The first person I met on the quay was my brother Michel, who without my knowing it had also gone to sea shortly after the war. He had arrived some weeks earlier in a Moroccan ship, which also was in a wretched state and in great need of repair. Although he had risen more quickly than I and had very good pay as second officer, he had left the ship almost at once.

He strongly advised me to follow his example, and described in glowing language the merry, free, delightful life in Tahiti. Twenty-four hours' leave convinced me that Tahiti was the right place for me too, and I immediately went to the owners' agent and asked to be allowed to sign off.

Unfortunately it appeared that the French shipping laws were rather different from the Moroccan, under which Michel had sailed, for the agent promptly read out a paragraph in my contract which made it clear that I was not entitled to sign off before we returned to Marseilles. The temptation was too great, and I made up my mind to desert. In most of the books of adventure I have read desertion is a most exciting and dangerous business—especially when it takes place in a tropical port—and every deserter is pursued by at least half a dozen armed men, of whom, of course, he is always able to rid himself, for example by plunging into a dark, exotic forest or disappearing into the crowd in a picturesque sailors' quarter. To tell the truth, my own desertion was much less dramatic: I simply sat on the verandah of a bar in pleasant company and saw my ship steam out of the harbour.

A few days later, when I felt safe, I reported to the authorities. To my great disappointment they did not appreciate my straightforwardness. I was tried in record time, sentenced to two months' imprisonment, and immediately placed under lock and key. Fortunately I was allowed to kill the time by reading, and my extremely mixed supply of literature included Herman Melville's book *Omoo*, which gives a most humorous description of how the author and several of his shipmates, on a visit to Tahiti a hundred years earlier, had also been sentenced for desertion and shut up in a 'calabooza' which had obviously stood on almost the same spot as my prison. If Melville is to be believed, he obtained his release in an unexpected manner: the Tahitian warder gradually grew tired of looking after the prisoners and therefore discreetly allowed them to disappear. Unfortunately times had changed, and my Tahitian warder, though pleasant and good-natured, never forgot to shut the door of the cell properly. I was obliged to leave Tahiti two months later in another of the company's ships without having seen much more of the island than a few bars, the court of justice and Papeete gaol.

I continued my wandering sailor's life for a few years longer, till it was time for me to do my military service. Although I was enrolled in the Navy, I was sent straight to Port Lyautey in Morocco, where for some unknown reason I was immediately put to drive a jeep. By a curious chance only a few months later my brother Michel began his somewhat belated military service in Casablanca, so at last we had an opportunity of getting to know each other a little better.

I was due to leave the service in a few days when, one morning at the beginning of February 1953, Michel rang up from Casablanca and told me that a French ship had just arrived which had a Tahitian crew and was on her way to Tahiti. He wanted me to come to Casablanca at once. I took this news a good deal more calmly than Michel, and was by no means as convinced as he was that the captain and crew would be particularly interested in a meeting with us. Nevertheless I took the bus to Casablanca when I next got leave.

The Tahitian vessel proved to a motor-ship of a little over 100 tons and was called *Kaumoana* (which I discovered later was not actually a Tahitian, but a Tuamotuan name). The crew most certainly consisted of merry Tahitians, who not only provided a regular feast for us, with raw fish, boiled bananas, roast pork and red wine, but also entertained us with guitar music and songs from their distant native island. I do not know if the red wine or the melancholy and nostalgic songs were most to blame, but when we went ashore from *Kaumoana* early in the morning we both had a violent longing to return to Tahiti. We plodded meditatively along the quays. Michel had still several months to serve. But I should certainly be able to get away before *Kaumoana* sailed.

I had made no plans for the future whatever. So there was nothing to prevent me from returning to Tahiti—if only I could get permission to join *Kaumoana*. Four days later I was back in Casablanca in civilian clothes. *Kaumoana* was still lying at the quay, and the owner, who had just bought the ship in France and was now taking her to Tahiti himself, was on board. With a thumping heart I explained what my business was. The owner listened to me amiably, but told me at once that he could engage no more seamen. My spirits fell: but after long and profound thought he added quite unexpectedly that perhaps I might come as a non-paying passenger if I was willing to take a watch. Of course this was only a rather more roundabout and elegant way of saying that he did not mean to pay me any wages. But what did that matter? I was afraid of his changing his mind and accepted at once.

Apart from the owner being so seasick that not only he, but all the rest of us on board, really thought he would die, all went well as far as Martinique, in the West Indies. The original intention had been that we should refuel there, but when the owner heard that diesel oil was much cheaper in Panama he decided to proceed there at once, the engineer having declared that we had more than enough oil left for this short voyage. The owner's calculation was far from stupid, and the chief engineer's measurement was correct. But neither of them had considered that there are often violent gales in the Caribbean Sea, and that in such circumstances a ship consumes much more oil than usual. And of course a gale was just what we met with. When on the third day it at last began to moderate, the chief engineer came clambering up on deck and announced with a blank face that we had just enough oil for another half-hour at half speed. We were still more than 100 miles from Panama. The captain, whose advice was now asked at last, had the engine stopped and rigged up an improvised sail with a tarpaulin. We did not go fast, but we could at least keep a course.

After two anxious days we sighted, at nine in the evening, the flash of the lighthouse at the entrance to the Panama Canal. The captain was delighted: he set the engine going and steered into the basin which, according to his manual of sailing directions, was just inside the lighthouse. Presumably there had been a basin there when the manual was published. But that, as subsequent inquiry showed, was in 1914, and at any rate when we arrived the harbour had quite a different layout. Unfortunately we did not discover this before a nasty scraping noise was suddenly heard under the keel. When it grew light the owner sent for a diver, who immediately discovered that the propeller was seriously damaged.

There were two ship-repairing yards in the Panamanian twin towns of Cristobal and Colón, one smart and hyper-modern in the American zone, and another dirty and old-fashioned in the part which belonged to the Republic of Panama. The American yard was dear and one had to pay in dollars. In the Panamanian yard the prices were considerably lower and one could pay in easily obtainable balboas. This decided the matter. *Kaumoana* was laboriously hauled up on to the slip in the Panamanian yard and entrusted to a gang of dark-faced men in dirty overalls, who seemed anything but contented at having been compelled to break off an animated game of cards.

The yard had assured us that the repairs would not take more than a few days. In fact they took a whole fortnight, which all the shipping agents in Panama thought extraordinarily quick work. We took possession of our ship again, as happy as a party of schoolboys on an outing, and chugged off through the canal. We were soon rolling in the heavy swell of the Pacific on our way to the Galapagos Islands, our last port of call before Tahiti. But we had been no more than two days at sea when the chief engineer came up on deck again with the same deep wrinkles on his forehead which we had seen at the time of our earlier mishap in the Caribbean Sea. This time it was the shaft bearing that had become overheated. The chief engineer strongly advised the owner and the captain to return to Panama and put it right while there was still time, and after some hesitation they agreed to do so.

No more was needed to make the bearing cool down

at once. Several hours passed. The motor was still working faultlessly. The longer they listened to the level beat of the engine, the more the chief engineer, the captain and the owner were agreed that it would be a fearful waste of money and time to have a bearing repaired when there was obviously nothing wrong with it. The owner, visibly relieved, finally ordered that the ship should turn round again and continue her voyage. Notoriously, a motor can be as capricious as a woman, so in the first hours after we had resumed our westward course we feared every moment to hear new and depressing bulletins from the engine-room. But these, to our astonishment, did not come.

On the other hand, there now seemed to be something wrong *above* decks, for the captain and mate began hurrying anxiously in and out of the owner's cabin. Of course it was not long before we found out what was happening. The owner had suddenly been taken ill: that is to say, he was not merely seasick, as he had been ever since we left Casablanca, but was also suffering from a violent colic. Or could it be iliac passion? No one really knew. The only thing that was certain was that his condition was rapidly becoming worse. It was obvious that he needed more efficient and expert care than anyone on board could give him. The only place where he could get expert medical treatment was Panama. So we turned round once more and went back at full speed.

We tried to relieve the owner's pain in every conceivable way, but he gradually grew worse. The hospital at Panama was still at least twenty-four hours away.

The situation was desperate. But while I happened to be at the wheel the captain had an inspiration. Perhaps there was a doctor somewhere nearer, for example on the great peninsula which projected from the upper half of the isthmus of Panama on our port side? I was ordered to steer for the peninsula. In a short time a small and incredibly rusty and dirty coasting steamer, with smoke pouring from her funnel, crossed our bows. Feeling sure that her captain would be able to tell us where the nearest doctor lived, we at once began to pursue her. We were soon so close that we could distinguish both the flag and the men on board. She was Nicaraguan. Some of the men—presumably the captain and mates—seemed to have their eyes fixed to long telescopes and to be staring uninterruptedly in our direction.

One of our officers had just begun to look at the Nicaraguans through the ship's binoculars. He suddenly burst out: 'Good God, those aren't telescopes in their hands, they're rifles!'

The unhappy Nicaraguans evidently thought that a new revolution had broken out in their country since they had left port and that we were revolutionaries intent on capturing their ship. As soon as we were within hearing distance, therefore, our captain stepped out on to the deck with true contempt for death, seized a megaphone and tried to explain our tragic situation in a language which he hoped was Spanish. For a long time the Nicaraguans stared at us mistrustfully, with rifles at the ready, but at last one of them pointed north-eastward and bellowed: 'Doctor, doctor, Coiba.' On looking at our chart we found that there was in fact a large island called Coiba in those parts, only twenty-five miles away. We gave the Nicaraguans a cheer and turned our bows towards Coiba.

When at last we arrived there it was evening, and pitch dark. After a while we could vaguely make out a small patrol boat and three or four canoes rapidly approaching us. Before we realized what was happening the deck was swarming with bare-footed soldiers pointing their guns threateningly at our stomachs. Now it really looked as if we had got into a revolution in earnest, evidently on the wrong side. We cursed the Nicaraguans who had played this dirty trick on us. But perhaps they had really thought that we were pirates of some kind. Our captain, who had now had good practice, managed to explain what we wanted quite well, but the only reply was an angry shout in English from the patrol boat:

'Coiba is a Panamanian convict settlement. The whole island is full of murderers. Landing here is absolutely forbidden. Clear off at once!'

We had had another extraordinary stroke of ill-luck. The captain very sensibly decided to get out of the harbour as quickly as possible, and caught hold of the wheel himself to swing the vessel round. Our manoeuvre was interrupted by a new order from the commander of the patrol boat. He now wanted us to wait until the doctor of the convict settlement had examined us to find out whether we were speaking the truth. In astonishingly quick time a canoe came out with the doctor on board. After a hurried and casual examination of the owner—who fortunately looked very ill and weak—he declared to our relief that it certainly was a serious case, but that he happened to have the right medicine for it. When an orderly brought it on board a little later it proved to be a bunch of green coconuts. Immediately after this the commander of the patrol boat gave us permission to continue our voyage, and we made use of it without losing a second.

We had no great confidence in the prison doctor's peculiar medicine, but anyhow we opened a nut and forced the contents down the owner's throat. It was not long before we realized that the prison doctor was an unrecognized genius, who ought to be remembered at the next award of Nobel prizes. For only half an hour after the owner had consumed his first nut he felt better, and after three or four more nuts he was quite cured of his mysterious gastric complaint—which may really have been nothing more than simple constipation. Even his seasickness was so much better next day that he was able to sit in a chair on deck for several hours. But of course it returned by degrees with its usual violence.

Four days later we reached the Galapagos Islands, where we cast anchor in a bay with the ominous name Wreck Bay. The engine, however, had ceased to give trouble a long time before, and in other respects our vessel seemed to be in perfect order, so that no one had any gloomy presentiments. When we had filled our water tanks, we said goodbye without regret to the giant tortoises, the convicts and the crazy freaks who were the only inhabitants, and set a course for Tahiti. For a long time we seemed really to have left all cares and troubles behind us. The Pacific really justified its name, for the waves rolled on in level succession, and the distances between them was so great that we glided over them quite imperceptibly. The sun shone with just a pleasant warmth. We stripped almost naked and enjoyed life to the full. I began to wish that our lovely holiday voyage might last for ever. I had hardly formed this wish before it looked like being fulfilled. As usual, the chief engineer's worried expression and unusual hurry revealed that all was not well below decks. Of course that wretched bearing had overheated again. To be exact, it was red-hot.

The captain had a long and thorough discussion with the chief engineer and the owner, and at last the trio agreed to continue the voyage at all costs. I thought their decision right and wise, as did all on board. The trade winds were blowing without cessation from east to west, i.e., in the direction in which we were travelling. The ocean currents too were flowing the right way. So that even if the bearing broke up altogether and the engine stopped, we should certainly be able to work our way forward to our destination by rigging up a sail again.

The bearing continued to overheat several times a day with astonishing regularity, but the engineers prevented it from going to pieces by cursing loudly and by diligently pouring water over it. If curses and water did no good, they simply stopped the engine for a few hours.

So we gradually came to regard our fitful and capricious method of progression almost as normal, and did not worry about it any more.

On April 25th we had covered two-thirds of the distance between the Galapagos Islands and Tahiti. A little after noon we made one of our usual stops to let the bearing grow cool. When an hour or two later the chief engineer considered that it was safe for us to proceed, the motor started at once. But something happened that was unusual and peculiar; *Kaumoana* refused to move. The captain gave an emphatic order for full speed ahead: but *Kaumoana* merely continued to bob up and down on the same spot. The captain conceived a horrible suspicion, and as if instinct told him that I shared it and was therefore the very man for the job, he ordered me to jump into the water and inspect the propeller. I put on a mask and a breathing tube and slid down a rope which the captain had made fast astern. One glance below the surface was enough for me to see what was wrong. We had lost our propeller! The shaft was quite undamaged, so the only explanation of the misadventure was that the shipyard workers in Panama had forgotten to insert the cotter pin or had inserted it so carelessly that it had fallen out.

The chart showed that we were only 250 miles from the Marquesas Islands and not much farther from the nearest atoll in the Tuamotu group. If we rigged up a couple of simple sails, we should surely be able to reach one of these groups of islands in a few days. But what would happen when we did arrive? The Marquesas

Islands had all high, inaccessible, rocky coasts, and those of the Tuamotu group had only narrow entrances, hard to navigate, or no entrances at all. Our steering capacity was extremely small, and we could not beat up against the wind, so it would be a hare-brained, if not impossible, enterprise to try to put in to one of these islands. What we needed was undoubtedly a tug, and the sooner we got it the better. The captain, loudly praising his own foresight, produced a large and handsome wireless transmitter and eagerly began to call up Papeete and the Taiohae station in the Marquesas group. Whichever way he screwed and turned the knobs, he could not get a sound. But it was not till towards the following morning that he gave it up and began to consider whether there was not some other way of getting us out of the nasty hole we were in. He soon saw that the only thing he could do was to launch the ship's boat and send some of the crew off to Taiohae to ask for help. He decided to carry out this plan without delay, formed us up on deck and asked all volunteers to step forward.

I offered myself at once: not at all, if truth be told, because I felt any more herioc than my companions in misfortune, but impelled rather by an egoistic instinct of self-preservation. I was convinced that I should have a much better chance of survival if I joined the party in the easily managed ship's boat than if I stayed behind on board the clumsy *Kaumoana*. One of the mates, three Tahitian seamen and an engineer, who had evidently come to the same conclusion as myself, also stepped forward. Having hastily stowed away some provisions and water, we cast off and hoisted our sail. A steady following wind carried us quickly away from *Kaumoana,* and we were soon alone on the sea.

When the great warm sun rose above the horizon two days later we were relieved and at the same time alarmed to find ourselves quite close to a high rocky island, which could only be Uahuka, in the Marquesas group. At the same time the wind died away quite suddenly and incomprehensibly. We had no choice but to dip our oars and row for dear life.

According to the chart it was over thirty miles from Uahuka to Taiohae in Nukuhiva, where the radio station was. We eloquently assured one another that it was only a temporary calm and toiled away at the oars. But hours passed and not a breath of wind ruffled the glassy surface of the sea. We suffered terribly from the heat. Our hands were cruelly split and torn. As we went on rowing dully and mechanically we sank by degrees into a kind of trance, which lasted till the cool of twilight brought us to ourselves again and we found that we had almost reached Taiohae Bay. A few flickering paraffin lamps showed where the village lay. But now we became conscious again of the pain in our lacerated hands and the ache in our long-suffering backs, and when at last we heard the sound of the boat scraping on the beach it was like the sweetest music in our ears. We crawled out more dead than alive and staggered off towards the lights. About halfway to the village we met two men.

'Oh, there you are at last,' one of them said cheerfully.

'We don't want to hear any stupid jokes,' groaned the mate.

'Our ship's lost her propeller and we've sailed and rowed here to get help,' I explained in a faint voice.

'We know all about it,' man number two interrupted me. 'The radio man here at Taiohae got into touch with *Kaumoana* half an hour after you'd started. So your little sail has really been quite unnecessary.'

They both laughed long and heartily.

We would have liked to murder them on the spot, but unfortunately we were much too weak and exhausted to deal with them: and really, when we came to think of it, it was not their fault that the wireless had not worked earlier.

But why had it been so long before *Kaumoana* had been able to establish contact with Taiohae? Luckily for our peace of mind we got no answer to this question till the day after, when we had pretty well recovered. The explanation was as simple as unexpected. All the wireless telegraphists in the whole of French Polynesia had been on strike for a week past to get higher wages, and it was by pure chance that the administrator at Taiohae had picked up *Kaumoana*'s wavelength while looking for a short-wave station with jazz music. A schooner which had just arrived at Taiohae had gone out at once to rescue our drifting comrades. She returned in triumph the very next day with *Kaumoana* in tow. It could not be denied that our heroic exertions had been absolutely unnecessary.

Kaumoana, then, was safe in Taiohae Bay, but how

and when she was to be repaired no one really knew. As I was formally still only a passenger I felt that I was fully entitled to abandon the owner and his companions in misfortune at once and jumped on board the copra schooner when she left Taiohae immediately afterwards. A week later I was in Papeete at last, and this time I was a free man.

It took me only a week or two to find out that life in Tahiti was not quite as carefree and simple as I had imagined. One could not settle down anywhere one liked under the palm-trees, for all the land had owners and was divided, enclosed and fenced round at least as thoroughly as in Europe. It was not a fact that all the trees were groaning with ripe fruit which could be picked free of charge. Although the lagoon swarmed with brilliantly coloured fish, it was almost impossible for a poor European, who had not the natives' thorough knowledge of where and how to fish, to catch any. It was evident that the money I had saved would not last long and that the most sensible thing for me to do was to look for a job at once. But despite all this I was not disappointed, for life was interesting and different from what I had known, the climate was delicious, and the inhabitants extraordinarily good-natured and full of fun. What more could I ask? Especially as the Tahitian women fully deserved their reputation of being the most charming, seductive and frivolous in the world.

When I had parted with all my money, I shipped as a seaman on board a copra schooner. It was hard and monotonous work, continually loading and unloading hundredweight sacks of rancid copra or vanilla with its sickly sweet smell, but we were well paid for our toil each time we called at a new island. Everywhere in the hundred islands of French Polynesia a visit from a schooner was a great and rare event, so wherever we went we were met with song and dance and general jollification.

What finally made me abandon my free roving sailor's life and stay for eight whole months on Rurutu, one of the Austral Islands, was not women, but the sight of a vegetable garden there. Nowhere in the world had I seen such large and perfect melons, radishes and lettuces as on this island. Here, I told myself, as I walked to and fro among the plantations, was the solution of all my financial problems. There was a shortage of vegetables in Papeete and consequently prices were high. If I did not want someone else to get in ahead of me, I had better start planting and exporting to Tahiti at once. Before I went to sea I had often helped my various foster-parents to grow vegetables, so I was not by any means so ignorant and inexperienced as might be thought. I tried to put my plans into execution at once. To rent a piece of land was easy enough. All the vegetables I planted did well and grew splendidly. The harvest which I gathered in a few months later was a record. So far everything was surpassing my expectations.

Unfortunately I had overlooked a small but important detail. There was no reliable, quick and regular communication with Tahiti. The schooners had seldom any cargo space available for my vegetables, and if by chance they ever were able to take them they cruised about in the Austral group for so long that the vegetables were rotten when they arrived at Papeete. But I had to pay the freight in any case. My ambitious project collapsed like a house of cards, and I left Rurutu a disappointed man by the first schooner that came along. I could not remember having seen her before, but none the less she seemed strangely familiar. Suddenly it dawned on me. She was my old ship, the unlucky *Kaumoana*, newly repaired and reconstructed so as to be almost unrecognizable.

Among the passengers on board was a native from the Marquesas Islands who for one reason or another needed money and was therefore on his way to Papeete to sell a copra plantation. I realized at once how stupid I had been to try my hand at anything so new-fangled as vegetable growing. Of course the only thing by which one could make money in French Polynesia was copra. The nuts fell down of themselves, and it was easy to take out the meat and dry it in the sun. Copra, too, was not injured in transport, while the relatively high price was guaranteed by a special fund.

Alas, I had not even the surprisingly modest sum which was needed to buy the Marquesan's copra plantation. But as always in my life when my need has been greatest, my brother Michel was at hand, for only a few days later I met him in the street in Papeete quite unexpectedly. He had finished his military service a long time before, but had not wanted to return to Tahiti earlier, considering that he ought first to earn a decent sum of money as starting capital. I embraced him with quite special cordiality and gave him a rapid account of the splendid deal which a person with a fair supply of capital should be able to bring off if only he acted promptly. Michel produced the sum required without a moment's hesitation and made me his partner on very favourable terms. In the best of spirits we took a schooner up to the Marquesas Islands with our new contract in our baggage. A few weeks later we were on our way back to Tahiti, downcast and disappointed. In a sense, the seller had not swindled us, for our land was certainly there and there were plenty of palms on it. But we were swindled none the less, for the land was situated on a hillside so steep that it could without exaggeration be said to stand on edge. Only wild goats could keep a footing on it, and to crown everything it ran right down to the sea, so that all the nuts fell into the water.

On our return to Papeete Michel immediately obtained a good post as mate of a motor ship which plied regularly between Tahiti and the neighbouring phosphate island Makatea. I myself was just about to sign on with another copra schooner when my brother returned from one of the uneventful routine trips which he now made twice a week and told me eagerly that the post of assistant harbour-master on Makatea was vacant. According to Michel I was just the sort of man for the job. I considered my position. I was already twenty-three and it was time that I gave some thought to the future. This was certainly a job with a future. I applied for the post, without any great hope of getting it. To my surprise and, I think, Michel's too, I got it.

Time passed. I seemed to be doing my work to the general satisfaction. I had a more comfortable and more pleasant life than I had ever had before. But nevertheless I gradually became strangely restless, and before two years had passed I began to look longingly after every ship which left 'my' harbour.

Once more it was Michel who gave my life a new direction.

Chapter 2

EASTWARD BOUND

Michel was on one of his usual weekly visits to Makatea, and he and I were sitting together and chatting about one thing and another. After quite a while he mentioned in a casual way that he had just decided to accompany Eric de Bisschop on a voyage to South America by raft. I was by no means sure that I had really heard him aright, and asked him to repeat what he had said. He told me again of his strange decision, as quietly as ever, and added that he had already given his employers notice. I was speechless with astonishment and could not utter a word for a long time. I had often heard of Eric during my stay on Rurutu, where he had lived a long time before me, and I had read several books about his adventurous journeys. To me he was a remote, wonderful legendary figure, fully comparable with Magellan, Cook and Laperouse, and the daring voyage which he now proposed to undertake at the age of sixty-six seemed to me at least as magnificent and fantastic as the explorations of his more famous predecessors in the Pacific hundreds of years before.

Michel gave a brief account of the preparations which had just begun in earnest. Eric had already completed a sketch showing the structure of the raft in detail. The naval commandant in French Polynesia had kindly allotted space for her construction in the little naval dockyard at Papeete and promised all possible help. Friendly Tahitians had cut 800 thick bamboos. But Eric's labour force was still quite inadequate, for it consisted at present only of Michel, a common friend named Francis Cowan, who was also to take part in the voyage, and a few Tahitians whose duties and ideas were still rather vague. If they did their work well they would certainly be taken on for the voyage, Michel added. It was easy to understand what he was driving at. Instead of asking me straight out if I would like to take part in the expedition, he said goodbye immediately afterwards and sauntered down to the harbour, where his vessel was waiting.

Michel's tactics were clever. If he had tried to persuade me to go with him, I should have resisted him instinctively and found a number of weighty reasons for remaining on Makatea, where I had at last both economic security and a good chance of promotion. But now, shrewdly enough, he had merely dropped a hint and set my imagination working. Evidently he knew better than myself how powerful an ex-sailor's longing for the sea can be. Almost against my will my thoughts began more and more often to dwell on the wonderful adventures in which Michel was to participate, but not I. At last I capitulated and accepted the seductive offer which, in fact, no one had yet made to me.

When I arrived at Papeete at the beginning of June 1956, I found Michel and Francis busily engaged in binding bamboos as thick as a man's arm into huge bundles. When Eric turned up a little later to see how the work was going, he did not seem in the least surprised at my presence and only gave me an encouraging pat on the back. Evidently Michel had assured him a long time before that he could count on me. At any rate Eric's behaviour seemed to indicate that I was accepted as a member of the expedition and I set to work with vigour. As soon as we completed a bundle of bamboos we placed it in a huge wooden frame, 45 feet long and 6 feet wide. Upon this huge floating body a raised deck with two masts and a cabin were to rest. Thus the construction could hardly have been simpler in principle, but it was not long before we were tired to death of sitting astride bamboos in the oppressive tropical heat and binding, pulling and making knots.

When the secretary of the expedition, Carlos Garcia-Palacios, who was also Chilean Consul in French Polynesia, appeared with a square-built little Chilean who, he declared, was willing to help us, we therefore accepted the offer with delight. In reply to our inquisitive questions Carlos told us that Juanito Bugueño, as his countryman was called, was a ship's engineer by trade, and had arrived ten months before on board a Chilean yacht. During his stay in Tahiti the owner of the yacht had received an advantageous offer from a business firm in Papeete and sold her. Instead of returning home to Chile at once, as the rest of the crew had done, Juanito had spent his passage money on a long series of wonderful parties with his newly acquired Tahitian girl friends. But nothing lasts for ever, and least of all money in Tahiti. Consequently poor Juanito soon had neither money nor girl friends. For the last few months he had been working in the consul's garden, an arrangement of which both parties were now tired. Juanito could not speak a word of French, but we showed with eloquent gestures what we expected of him. Smiling cheerfully, as if we had done him a favour, he immediately sat down astride a few bamboos and began to bind them together with such speed and skill that it almost looked as if he had done nothing else all his life.

We were all soon happily agreed that (1) Juanito was worth good recompense for his work (2) that the best recompense we could give him was to let him join our expedition.

We spoke to Eric about it, and as another man who had been thought of as a participator had just refused, he agreed at once to enrol Juanito. Perhaps, Eric added, we should have a use for his skill as a mechanic right away, as we were going to take a complete radio outfit with us, with a petrol engine and everything. Juanito laughed as usual, without understanding a word. I do not know exactly when he realized that he had risen in rank and had been appointed a member of the expedition, but at any rate he never made any attempt to avoid the dubious honour. The chief reason for that, as we discovered later, was certainly that the authorities had refused to prolong his *permis de séjour*.

We got through our work so well that we were able to launch the raft as early as the beginning of September. We named her at her launching *Tahiti Nui*, which means 'great Tahiti' and is the natives' ancient and proud name for their island. The raft attracted an attention which was well justified, not only by reason of her appearance but also because she rode the water with the utmost grace and ease. One of the most sceptical visitors to the yard during her building was Thor Heyerdahl, who was paying only a short visit to Papeete on his way home from his archaeological excavations on Easter Island. He shook his head seriously and solemnly declared that he would never dare to entrust his life to such a fantastic craft. But, when one came to think of it, Thor Heyerdahl was not a sailor at all, and so my faith in Eric remained unshaken. It was further strengthened during the most successful trial trip which we made at the beginning of October. Like all my comrades on the expedition—Eric, Michel, Francis and Juanito—I looked forward with the greatest confidence to the voyage of over 5000 miles which lay before us.

Eric had estimated that the voyage would take between three and four months, but to be on the safe side we had stowed away on board enough flour, rice, biscuits, preserves and other food-stuffs for five months. Despite this many of our friends in Tahiti evidently feared for our well-being, for they came on board at the last moment with beer bottles, hams and parcels of food of every conceivable kind. A few kind people even had the ingenious idea of giving us a dozen live fowls, a live sow and a particularly durable iron ration in the shape of 200 coconuts, whose holes were carefully stopped with breadfruit resin in the Tahitian style. We were also provided with three kittens as mascots.

When we left Papeete on November 8, 1956, our raft as seen from outside looked more like a Noah's ark than anything (this impression was strengthened by her having been decorated with flowers and leaves from stem to stern by a party of Tahitian women), while the interior of the cabin most suggested a well-assorted grocer's shop during the annual stocktaking. But we did not care in the least what the raft looked like, nor did we worry at all about the fearful disorder which prevailed everywhere. On the other hand, we did begin to feel acutely uneasy at our raft having become several tons heavier as the result of this unanticipated generosity. The observations of two days and nights convinced us that we must either throw some of the cargo overboard or put back to Tahiti and increase the raft's buoyancy by filling up the empty space between the floats and the deck with bamboos. Eric was reluctant to part with valuable provisions and therefore decided to put back. It was pretty clear that an about turn so soon after the start would give rise to many malicious rumours and jests, and I admired him for his contemptuous indifference to this unpleasant prospect.

As we had difficulty in tacking against the wind in spite of our centreboards, we took out our wireless transmitter and asked the naval commandant at Papeete to send out the gunboat (which had towed us out of Papeete harbour) to fetch us in again. She arrived twelve hours later and mercifully took us to a remote creek on the south coast of Tahiti, where we quickly collected several hundred bamboos and bound them fast below decks. This did the trick. Much relieved at not having to get rid of any provisions—which in the long run we might be very glad to have—we resumed our southward course as soon as the gunboat had towed us outside the coral reef.

Between Tahiti and the westerly winds at a latitude of 40° south, which sailors aptly call the 'roaring forties' on account of their violence, easterly winds of varying strength prevail for the most part. We were therefore prepared for the first part of the voyage, till we got down to 40° south, being the most difficult. But to our great satisfaction we almost immediately found a strong following wind which lasted for a whole week. It was replaced by a north-easterly wind, which certainly made us lose some degrees of longitude, but on the other hand it helped us to put several degrees of latitude behind us, which was the most important thing. Unfortunately our good luck came to an end when we were on a level with the Austral Islands, and for many days, to our disgust, we drifted slowly but surely backwards in the neighbourhood of Raivavae, the island on which Eric had lived for the past two years as land surveyor. When the unwelcome contrary wind ceased we were due north of the island after having described an almost perfect semi-circle round its eastern half. We therefore completed the circle by steering down along the west coast of the island as soon as the weather allowed it, and several times caught sight of the high cliffs. Eric's eyes remained fixed on the island which had been his last home till it disappeared into the sea, and his face wore an unusually gentle expression.

Next day we were participants in a new and much more amusing farewell. The Government schooner *Tamara,* which happened to be on a tour of inspection in the Austral group, came in sight. We were not altogether unprepared for this, as we had been in wireless contact with her earlier. The captain informed us with a serious countenance that he had orders from the governor to tow us back to Tahiti at once if we expressed the slightest wish for him to do so. We thanked him cordially for his kind offer and explained that the only thing we wanted was a little more water, wine and cigarettes, as we were not quite sure that our supply of these vital necessities would last all the way to Chile. The obliging captain complied with our request at once, after which he blew a long farewell on his siren and slowly withdrew, while his Tahitian sailors solemnly waved us goodbye, evidently convinced that they would never see us again. A few days later we crossed the latitude of the last and southernmost of the Austral Islands, Rapa. The whole of French Polynesia, with all its lovely islands and familiar waters, now lay behind us. Before us stretched the cold grey sea, empty and desolate, all the way to South America, 5000 miles farther east.

As early as the beginning of January 1957, i.e., only seven weeks after we left Tahiti, we encountered steady westerly winds at 33° south. This was a good deal farther north of what we had reckoned upon, but of course we were glad of it and set our course direct for South America. Our comfortable, seldom interrupted progress with a following wind, in more or less the same latitude, continued for nearly two months, the weather was good and the temperature kept between 68° and 77° Fahrenheit. (It was, of course, full summer in the southern hemisphere at this time.) The raft almost steered herself with the help of the centreboards and was highly satisfactory in safety and comfort. Watches, changes of sail, wireless contacts and cooking were easily done, and we had more time off than ever before either ashore or at sea.

Eric spent all his free time in reading his oceanographical and anthropological books and in making notes for the treatise on Polynesian navigation which he had long been planning to write. As usual he lived in another world, took all annoyances with Olympian calm and for long periods seemed so occupied with his own thoughts that he did not even notice what was going on round about him.

Francis's chief interest was fishing, and he could sit on deck for hours with his Tahitian fishing spear in his hand, on the look out for dolphins and tunny. Despite this his catches were very meagre, but this was only because there were so few fish in those latitudes, for Francis had been born and brought up in Tahiti and was at least as skilful a fisherman as the natives.

When our wireless operator Michel had sent his daily weather reports to Tahiti he often amused himself by picking up wireless fans all the world over, and several of these lived as far off as Syria and Norway. Or he produced the underwater gun which his Chinese judo pupils had given him before we left Tahiti, and jumped into the sea to fish, but was no more successful than Francis.

I myself took lessons in navigation from Eric and constructed a model canoe which I hoped would some day be the prototype for a full scale vessel of the kind. For many years I had dreamed of making long voyages in the Polynesian archipelago in an outrigger canoe.

Juanito, who was our cook, spent all his off-time learning a French dictionary by heart. His first attempt at reading a French book, however, was a complete fiasco, because he chose a thriller full of criminal's slang, which of course he could not find in his dictionary. After that he preferred to let us teach him and quickly learned an incredible number of everyday words and phrases—most of which were likewise not in his dictionary.

I must apologize for having forgotten a few of the members of the expedition who had unlimited time off from our sailing to our arrival—the sow and the cats. We had soon decided to spare the sow, which Juanito had christened Chanchita, till we had grown tired of roast chicken. It was, therefore, more than a month before we began to cast longing eyes on Chanchita. At that time a fine cock still survived, and in our dilemma we decided to draw lots as to which of the two should be the first victim. Chanchita won and so obtained another week's grace. Just as we were preparing to slaughter her on the following Sunday, Michel for once happened to catch a dolphin, so of course we gorged ourselves on grilled fillets of fish instead of roast pork. Exactly a week later, when slaughter day had come round again, Michel, incredible as it may sound, caught another dolphin.

This event looked like a sign from the hand of fate that we were to let Chanchita live. We and particularly Juanito had by this time become very fond of her, and therefore decided to treat her in future as a member of the expedition. Instead of having to live on leavings, as before, she now, in her new capacity of a full-blown member of the expedition, had her own helping at every meal. It was, for that matter, in our own interest to see that Chanchita was well fed, for as soon as she was hungry she always showed her dissatisfaction in the same unpleasant way—by grubbing up the deck and eating the packets of bamboos on which we floated.

One of the three cats which we had on board as mascots died while we were still cruising round the Austral Islands. The two that remained fell into the sea time after time, and each time we saved them only at the last moment and with the greatest difficulty. At last they got their sea legs and a sailor's life semed to suit them as well as the rest of us.

As if Chanchita and the cats had not been enough, we discovered one day another party of most unexpected stowaways—a school of lagoon fish. We had no difficulty in identifying the fish, as long as a man's finger, which are called *nanue* in Tahitian and live only in and around the blocks of coral in shallow lagoons in the South Sea islands. They had evidently taken our raft for a block of coral just before we left our last harbour on the southern side of Tahiti, and had not discovered the mistake until it was too late. We often put on our masks and put our heads down into the water along the edge of the raft to see if the *nanue* fish were still hanging on, and each time they approached in close formation wagging their tails cheerfully. If a shark or other predatory fish came gliding by they immediately disappeared into the chinks between the bamboos, where they were in perfect safety. Presumably there were enough seaweed and small marine creatures on the underside of the raft for them to be in no danger of starvation, but to be on the safe side we now and then threw scraps of food to them.

On Saturday, February 23, 1957, we passed the 117th degree of longitude and so had reached exactly halfway. As we had left Papeete on November 8, 1956, this meant that the first half of the voyage had taken almost exactly three and a half months. This was certainly much longer than Eric had calculated, but on the other hand all the indications were that we should be able to cover the remaining 2500 miles in a considerably shorter time. In the last fortnight we had been doing about fifty miles a day, and normally the winds ought to increase in strength as the southern winter came nearer. We decided to celebrate the event with a particularly grand Sunday dinner, but immediately afterwards the wind freshened so much that during the next twenty-four hours we had little time to do other than attend to the sails and steer. We took this with complete equanimity, especially seeing that when we took the altitude of the sun at the time for the planned Sunday dinner it appeared that we had done no less than seventy miles in the last twenty-four hours. Still, as the hours passed we began to wish that our speed was not quite so great, for the raft creaked ominously in her joints and, although the sails were reefed, the masts quivered like tightly drawn piano strings. Still more disturbing was a queer thumping noise under the floor of the cabin. And suddenly we saw a bamboo emerge astern and sail away in our wake. But the sea was so disturbed and stormy that we could do nothing about the matter for the moment.

The wind did not drop till next day, and then it dropped so quickly that there was soon a dead calm. We jumped overboard at once and closely examined the raft below the water-line. We found to our relief that we had lost only a few of the extra bamboos which we had stuffed into the empty space below decks when we last called at Tahiti. All the rest of the bamboos and lashings seemed to be undamaged. We wedged the clattering bamboos fast, climbed on board again and sat down to wait for a wind. It was not long before the heavy rolling swell began to be rippled by gusts of wind. It was soon blowing a steady forty miles an hour—from the wrong quarter. We tried to tack against the wind, which was due east, but but soon found that by doing so we only drifted more quickly westward. We therefore struck sail altogether

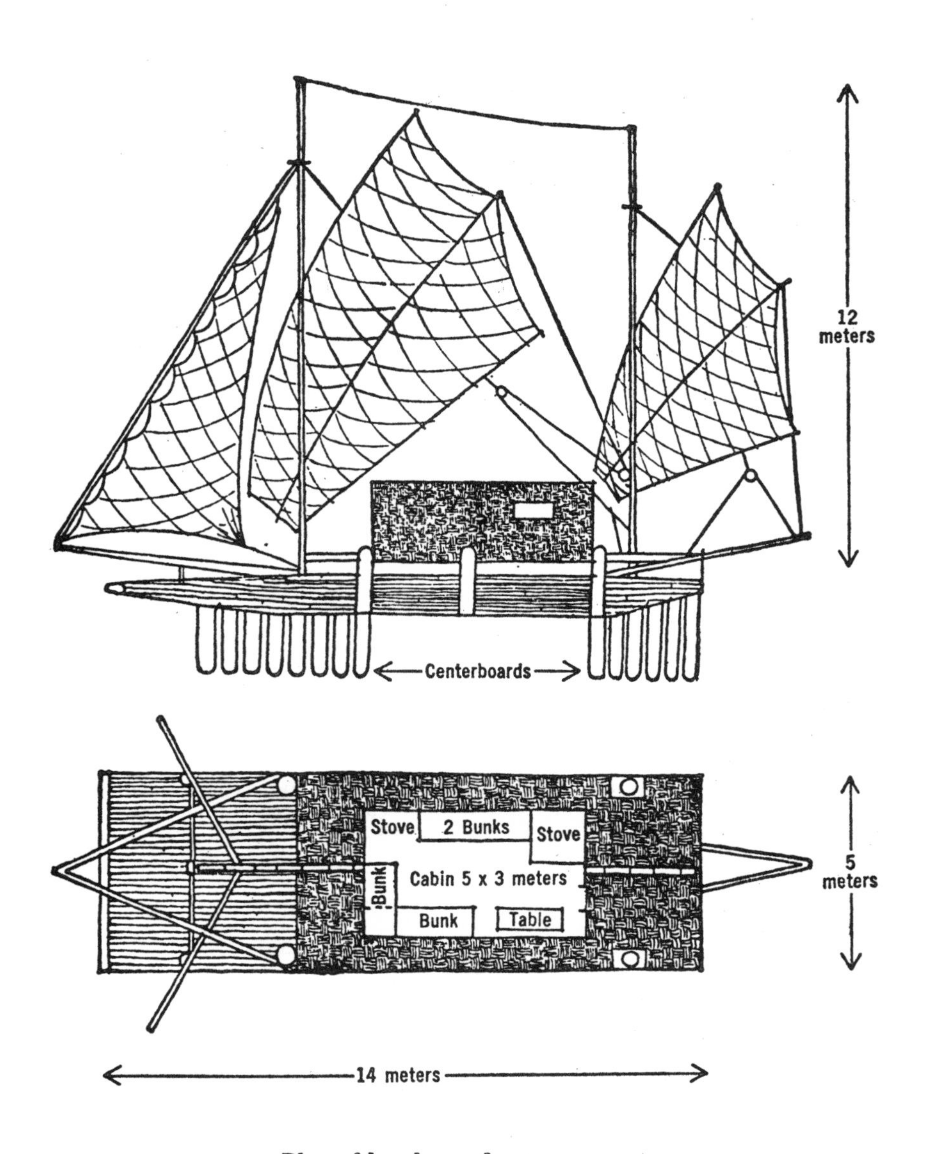

Plan of bamboo raft TAHITI NUI I
built for the voyage from Tahiti to Chile

and threw out a drogue made of a log of wood and a piece of canvas. This gave us some help.

The contrary wind lasted for a whole fortnight. Every day our position was moved back twenty, thirty or forty miles on the chart on the cabin bulkhead, and I often felt the same dull anger boiling up inside me as I had felt in my childhood when I was playing ludo and had to take back my piece and start again from the beginning. But now, unfortunately, I could not get out of it by upsetting the board or proposing another game. Every day one or two bamboos disappeared despite all our efforts to bind them securely. It did not matter so much in itself, as we we had now certainly consumed so much of our stores that the raft's reduced capacity to float was set off by her reduced weight, but it was extremely painful each time to see ourselves slowly drifting away from them as we moved back towards Tahiti.

On March 8th the wind shifted from east-south-west to north-north-east, and we hoisted sail again to try at least to get down to a more southerly latitude. On March 11th we completed our circle and passed exactly the same point where we had been seventeen days earlier, on February 23rd. So we were still only half-way across. Next day there was a dead calm, and we all wondered anxiously what kind of surprise there was in store for us this time. It was not till long after darkness had fallen that the first gust of wind came. We crowded expectantly round the binnacle and someone struck a match. There was no doubt about it. We actually had a fair wind, and while we were still standing round the binnacle, talking and chaffing one another, it rapidly increased in strength. A week later the wind was still blowing as evenly and steadily from the same quarter. We felt more and more convinced that our troubles were over at last.

But on March 21st, without any preliminary calm or other warning, the wind swung round quite unexpectedly from west to south, and then, a little later, to south-east. We tried to beat up against it as well as we could, but could not prevent the raft from taking a northerly course, up towards Easter Island. Eric, oblivious of everything else, plunged into profound speculation, and evolved the theory, particularly convincing in our situation, that this mysterious island had originally been discovered and peopled by Polynesian navigators who, like ourselves, had been driven off their course on a voyage to South America. I could not help wondering if it would not be a good idea to follow their example and make for harbour at Easter Island so that we might repair the raft. The nearest islands beyond Easter Island were Pitcairn in the west and Juan Fernandez in the east, and it was more than a thousand miles to either of them. Our only boat was a worn rubber dinghy, so small that it would not hold us all. The fact that we had a wireless was not much use to us either, for the chances of a vessel being in the neighbourhood, if we got into serious trouble in those lonely waters, were extremely small, and possibly nil. So Easter Island was certainly our only salvation if the raft began to sink.

But we never came within 300 miles of Easter Island,

for on April 3rd there was once more a strong favourable wind. So we had no choice but to go on towards Valparaiso. Before we sailed, it had been Eric's intention to go down at once to 40° south, where westerly winds prevail practically all the year round. Instead he had decided to swing eastward at 33° south, because we came upon favourable winds there. Everything had gone well for three and a half months, and all protests against Eric's decision had therefore died down. But now that we had lost more than five weeks in unnecessary wandering about we all felt a strong desire to go down to more southerly latitudes: at the same time we all saw, alas, that to do so would be sheer suicide on account of the wretched state of our raft. So we went on due east and tried to console ourselves with the thought that, according to all the laws of probability, we ought now, after our earlier setbacks, to have a fair wind for a long time to come.

It looked as if our faith in the laws of probability was justified, for during the next few weeks the fresh following wind not only continued but gradually increased in strength. Although now and then we saw a bamboo whirl away in our wake the raft did not seem to be sinking noticeably deeper, and at last we quite ceased to worry about these losses. Instead, our greatest anxiety all through April was for our water and food supply. For all our reckoning and rationing we could not see what we could do to make this last as far as Valparaiso, where in the most favourable event we could not arrive before the middle of June. The worst thing was that we had so little drinking water left. In the first months of our voyage it had rained so often that we had taken it for granted that we should always be able to replenish our supplies when necessary. But strangely, not a single drop of rain fell all through April. At the same time, for some curious reason, all the fish which had been accompanying the raft disappeared, so we could no longer count on keeping ourselves alive with fishes' blood when we had drunk the last drop of water.

'Don't you know that faith can work miracles? Spread out a piece of canvas and get out all our bottles and tanks,' Eric said with a knowing smile, one day towards the end of the month, when we were discussing our water problem with more anxiety than usual.

We looked up in astonishment at the blue sky, in which the sun was shining with a pleasant warmth, and burst into a roar of laughter. But, accustomed as we were to discipline at sea, we carried out our captain's order without making any objections. The same night thunder and lightning began, and in less than half an hour all our bottles and tanks were filled to the brim. Of course it was pure chance, but I am quite sure that Eric so regarded it. He certainly did not believe in God. But time after time chance occurrences of this kind had saved his life, and it seemed that he had gradually become convinced that he had been specially favoured by Fortune from his birth and therefore did not need to take any danger really seriously. It was certainly just this conviction that caused Eric time after time to take quite unnecessary risks with complete nonchalance.

At the beginning of May—our seventh month at sea—

the westerly wind became still stronger. We were still about a thousand miles from Valparaiso, and in our eagerness to arrive there as quickly as possible we set a couple of extra sails. It was a little rash, for we did not know how much strain the raft would stand, and we were examining her closely every day with ill-concealed anxiety. Curiously enough she seemed to be standing up to it well, and with each day that passed we became more and more hopeful.

But although we were still in happy ignorance of it, our worst trial was still ahead. The first warning of a gale came on the night between May 5th and May 6th, when I was suddenly awakened by a crash. At the same time the paraffin lamp, which we always left alight on the cabin table at night, went out. Still half asleep, I jumped down from my upper berth to see what was happening. I suddenly grew numb. I had water up to my knees. I snatched the electric torch which I kept under my pillow and let the cone of light sweep round the cabin. Furniture, clothes and books were floating in confusion in water eighteen inches deep, and astonished, sleepy faces peered from all the berths except that of Francis.

'It looks as if we're sinking,' said Eric quietly.

We all agreed more or less audibly, but for some reason we took this really most tragic discovery as calmly as Eric. Perhaps we had long ago become so accustomed to the idea that we had grown fatalistic. Or perhaps our lack of interest was simply due to the fact that we were too sleepy to react more vigorously. At any rate we were all still standing or sitting in the same positions, as if frozen, when a few seconds later Francis came wading into the cabin, bawling cheerfully.

'What's it like in the fish pond? There's nothing to worry about. But you'd better shut the after door in future if you want to sleep in peace.'

Francis told us in a few words what had happened. As we were now at last beginning to understand, a gigantic wave had come rolling over the sea from astern. We had seen hundreds of gigantic waves in the course of the voyage, and they had all lifted the raft high in the air and quietly rolled beneath her without even wetting the deck. This mysterious wave, on the contrary, besides moving much more quickly than any of the others, broke just before it reached the raft, and it was really due more to good luck than skill on his part that Francis succeeded in scrambling up the mast at the last moment. For a little while it looked as if the raft would remain waterlogged, but at last she rose out of the seething foam, shaking and trembling violently from the tremendous strain.

Of course we all regarded this episode as a sign that a storm was gathering, which after all was not surprising, as we were already some way into the southern winter. It is well known that one misfortune seldom comes alone, and Eric was unwell next day as a result of the drenching he had had in his lower berth on that disastrous night. Already several months before he had seemed so sensitive to cold and draughts that we had persuaded him—with some difficulty—not to take any more watches, and since we had passed the longitude of Easter Island at the beginning of April he had spent most of the time in his bunk.

A diligent perusal of our medical books had not enabled us to diagnose his difficulty in breathing and high temperature, so we came to the conclusion that he was simply worn out and exhausted. But after the misadventure with the mysterious wave it was not difficult to see that he was now also suffering from a severe chill.

It was now more than ever necessary to reach Chile quickly. As if at our request, the wind gradually increased in strength. Our joy, however, soon gave place to fear, for the strain seemed to be altogether too great for our poor raft, and although we struck all the sails but one the masts quivered like bowstrings. On May 7th we were compelled to strike even our last sail, a miserable little foresail. But we could not take down the cabin, and the wind pressed against it so violently that the raft soon took a list of forty-five degrees. It was no longer possible to walk upright, and as it was in any event no longer feasible to steer the raft we crept into the cabin again and hoped that the gale would at last continue to chase us on towards South America. Next day it moderated a little, and we peeped cautiously out through the cabin door. The masts were still there, but the deck was torn up on the starboard side, one of the beams which held the bamboos together was crushed and damaged bamboos stuck out into the water all round the raft.

We managed to repair the worst damage and set sail again. Helped by a fair wind of just the right strength we flew on towards Chile. A week passed. Our hopes rose. However, on May 16th the swiftly falling barometer warned us that a new storm was approaching, and to be on the safe side we immediately hauled down all the sails. This proved to have been a wise precaution, for only half an hour later we were in the middle of the worst storm I have encountered in all my life. The wind whistled ominously in the rigging, while the raft lurched and shook so violently that we tumbled over each other in the cabin. To crown all, this time we had met with an easterly gale, and so were on our way back to Tahiti. When, the following morning, the storm had moderated sufficiently for us to go out on deck again, we made a most alarming discovery: several of the big four-inch bamboos which formed the main body of the raft had broken loose and disappeared. Soon afterwards another bamboo came loose, and this time we managed to get hold of it before it fell off. We examined it curiously. It was full of large white ship-worms, and when we broke off a piece and as an experiment flung it into the sea it sank at once. It was evident that the raft would never hold out as far as Valparaiso, which was still 800 miles away, a distance which would take about sixteen days to cover. The nearest island of the Juan Fernandez group, Masafuera, on the other hand, was only 350 miles away. Perhaps we could get ashore there before the raft fell to pieces or sank altogether. But after a rather more thorough survey of our beloved *Tahiti Nui* we saw that we could not even reach this harbour of refuge without the assistance of a tug.

We had not yet been able to establish regular contact with any wireless fan in Chile, but our friend Roland d'Assignies in Tahiti was still answering our signals as promptly as ever. After a long discussion of the situation, therefore, we called him up late on the evening of Saturday, May 18th, and asked him to forward a telegram to the expedition's secretary, Carlos Garcia-Palacios, who had just reached Chile to prepare for our arrival. In the telegram we earnestly begged Carlos immediately to charter a boat which could tow us to Masafuera, and explained that it was our intention to proceed to Valparaiso without further help as soon as we had repaired the raft at that island. Roland read the telegram back to us and promised to forward it at once. While the raft was being tossed about helplessly on the rough sea we all turned in and had a good sleep so as to be in good fettle for the impending tow, which would certainly be extremely difficult.

Next day, Sunday, May 19th, when we turned on the wireless to hear if there was any answer from Carlos, we happened to pick up an American news bulletin, consisting mainly of politics and other matters of no interest to us whatever. Suddenly, to our astonishment, the announcer began to read a thrilling account of the tragic loss of the French raft *Tahiti Nui*. According to the communiqué, which the announcer gabbled in the cheerful tone reserved by all radio stations for particularly distressing incidents, the raft was completely smashed up and three of us seriously injured. But we heard a few seconds later that there was still hope, for on receiving our SOS the Chilean cruiser *Baquedano* had immediately gone out to rescue us despite the stormy weather. The announcer, with a strong sense of the dramatic, finished up by declaring triumphantly that we had fortunately been able to give our exact position, which considerably improved the chances of *Baquedano* finding us.

We stared at each other in amazement and burst into a roar of laughter, for such ludicrous nonsense we had not heard for a long time. But we soon became serious again. The false statements in the communiqué that we had sent out an SOS and that there were several injured on board the raft did not matter much. But much worse was that the position given by the announcer—32° south by 88° west—was quite different from our real one, which was 35° 05′ south by 89° 24′ west. It was easy to see what had happened. As unfortunately is often the case, some 'helpful' wireless fan had picked up our conversation with Roland and so utterly misunderstood it that he had been seized with panic and had immediately sent out a false alarm. It was indeed a pleasant situation.

Michel screwed wildly at all his knobs with the courage of desperation, and the incredible actually happened. For the first time in several months he made direct contact with a Chilean wireless fan, whose voice, moreover, was heard quite unusually clearly. Before we could point out all the absurd mistakes that had been made, he began to describe eagerly a new rescue operation being planned by the Chilean Air Force. It was as simple as it was bold. Two aircraft were to come out from the coast and drop rubber dinghies to us: we were to inflate these, clamber on board and wait quietly in them till the cruiser should arrive and pick us up. We hastened to assure our new friend that we were not in such imminent danger as he and everyone else in Chile seemed to think, and that it would be more than enough if we got the tow we had asked for. Of course we also begged him to see that the captain of *Baquedano* got our right position.

We turned off the wireless with a sigh of relief and sat down and tried to calculate how long it would take *Baquedano* to arrive. We came to the conclusion that it would be at least forty-eight hours. As we now had a moderate southerly wind again, we decided to set all sail and go to meet our rescuer. We were by no means sure that our raft, in her dilapidated condition, would stand towing for any length of time, and every extra mile we could put behind us considerably increased our chances of rescue. We hoped, with the help of the Chilean wireless fan, to be able to keep *Baquedano* informed of our position all the time. Next day, Monday, May 20th—incidentally our 193rd day at sea—we repaired our raft, which was still making a good speed, in a rough and ready fashion, and, according to an old seaman's tradition, cleaned ourselves up thoroughly. Our hopeful preparations seemed to give Eric new strength: he got up immediately and followed our example.

On Tuesday Michel at last made direct contact with *Baquedano,* and a careful calculation showed that we ought to meet between two and three o'clock next morning—if our last position was right, and our speed correctly estimated, which of course was far from certain. An error of only a few miles might lead to *Baquedano* missing us and our losing a precious day or two. It was therefore with a disagreeable premonition that I took the night watch and began to peer ahead for the rocking ship's lights which ought to be somewhere right ahead. But our navigation and *Baquedano*'s had evidently been irreproachable, for at 2:45 A.M. I detected a faint light on the eastern horizon. I hurried into the cabin to tell the good news to my shipmates, and found Michel at the wireless table engaged in a lively conversation with *Baquedano*'s wireless officer. Of course Michel did not fail to let him know that we were now in sight of each other. A few minutes later the Chileans turned on a powerful searchlight, and I replied with the rather more modest resources at our disposal—that is, by climbing up the mast and flashing an electric torch. Being uncertain where we should find time to have our next meal, we cooked ourselves a huge breakfast and attacked it with keen appetites.

Baquedano reached *Tahiti Nui* just after 4 A.M., and the captain launched a boat without waiting for dawn. When the boat approached us we saw by the light of our electric torches and lanterns that she was manned by seven men. The first of them to clamber on board had a Red Cross brassard round his arm. Before we could make out the next man's appearance and rank a powerful flashlight flared in our faces. He was obviously a photographer. The third was an officer, who seemed visibly disappointed at finding five well-dressed, freshly shaved men, who invited him to sit down at a well-furnished coffee table, instead of the same number of half-drowned, starving wrecks of humanity. Eric now felt so well that he decided to go back in the boat to discuss matters with *Baquedano*'s captain. He took Francis and Michel with him, while Juanito and I had the honour of taking over the command of *Tahiti Nui* for the time being.

Two hours later our comrades came back loaded with cigarettes, wine and provisions and told us of their experiences. At first the Chilean captain had wanted to abandon the raft and return to Valparaiso with us without delay. Eric, however, had been obstinate as usual, and at last the captain had agreed to try to tow the raft to the Juan Fernandez Islands, although he was convinced that it was impossible. Eric sat down at the cabin table with a look of triumph and sketched the new course.

Soon afterwards *Baquedano* came alongside and some cheerfully grinning sailors flung over the heavy tow-rope, which we had the greatest difficulty in picking up and making fast round a bollard in the bows. With beating hearts we watched the revolutions of *Baquedano*'s propellers increase and the rope slowly stretch. The raft then moved forward with a jerk and began uncertainly to follow the strange tug which was so much larger than herself. For once the weather was kind to us, and all would certainly have gone well if the two vessels had not been so ill-matched. The greatest problem was, of course, to maintain a speed which suited us both. *Baquedano*'s normal speed was twenty knots and only with the greatest difficulty could she maintain a speed of less than three knots. Our raft, on the other hand, began to creak in all her joints and play at being a submarine as soon as her speed exceeded two knots. But thanks to the Chileans' admirable patience and care there was no serious accident during the first twenty-four hours' towing, and our hopes rose.

They sank again on Thursday, however, as the barometer fell. The sea grew steadily rougher and more disturbed, and the raft shook and creaked horribly. Several large bamboos broke loose both on the starboard and on the port side. Just after midnight the tow-rope broke. But as we could not get hold of the two ends and splice them together before morning came, we all turned in to enjoy a few hours of much needed sleep. On Friday morning *Baquedano* came alongside, and the captain asked seriously if we really thought it worth while to continue the towing. When we replied that we did, he had a fresh rope flung over to us, but during this difficult manoeuvre our raft suddenly bumped into the ship's side. The whole of the starboard side was torn up and masses of bamboos came loose. As a result of this misadventure we took a heavy list, but we made the rope fast, nevertheless, and signalled to *Baquedano* to go ahead. Another day passed slowly. It was not difficult to see that the end was near. But we were now not more than 150 miles from Masafuera, and we could not bring ourselves to abandon our raft so long as a glimmer of hope remained.

On Sunday morning, May 26th, the tow-rope parted again, and shortly afterwards we received a friendly but firm wireless message from the captain of *Baquedano* saying that he was sorry, but he could make no further attempts to tow us. The cause was a rather ignominious one: his consumption of oil had been abnormally large on account of the slow towing, and he had only just oil enough left to reach Valparaiso if he proceeded at full speed immediately. He therefore ordered us to get ready to board *Baquedano* from the raft, as the sea was now too rough for him to send a boat over. With heavy hearts we collected our few belongings in watertight kit-bags. It was our 199th day at sea and evidently the last.

Baquedano returned, describing a wide curve, and approached slowly from astern on the lee side of the raft. The first rope which the Chileans flung over snapped with a loud crack as soon as we made it fast to one of the side-posts. The next attempt was equally unsuccessful, but the third rope stood the strain, and we were soon tied up to *Baquedano* by three stout hawsers. Now we had to be quick and get our things on board before we were drawn in and crushed against the pitching steel hull a mere ten yards away. Our rescuers smartly and skilfully flung across a few slender ropes, and we quickly tied these round our kit-bags. One after another they were hauled up over the big neighbour's rail, till only one remained. Juanito had got hold of this and was fiddling about with it in a corner of the fore-deck. What on earth was he doing? I gave a bellow of anger and rushed over to help him. As I did so I saw that it was not a sack he had between his legs but Chanchita, our sow.

'But you aren't going to leave her behind on board *Tahiti Nui*?' he said reproachfully.

No, of course we would not. But to tell the truth we had simply forgotten her existence. Juanito had already managed to fasten a life-belt round her stomach, and I helped him to tie it tight. Curiously enough the sow made no resistance, and when I tried to put her on her legs she was as feeble and lifeless as a marzipan pig.

'She's dying of fright, or there's something else wrong with her,' I burst out in astonishment. 'She was as fit and well as ever only this morning.'

'There's nothing wrong with her,' Juanito replied fiercely. 'But I gave her our last bottle of wine to quiet her a bit.'

By our combined efforts we heaved the intoxicated sow into the sea and signed to the sailors on board *Baquedano* to haul in. They evidently thought she was one of the members of the expedition who had collapsed and needed prompt medical treatment, for we saw the ship's doctor and two male nurses running up. But a concerted bellow from practically the whole crew of *Baquedano* soon told us that Chanchita was in safety and that her rescuers had discovered their mistake. Juanito, well content, stuffed the cats into a bag and held it tight under his arm.

Now it was our turn. As we had no great desire to follow Chanchita's example, we climbed up on to the cabin roof and bawled to the Chileans to try to haul us closer so that we could jump when a wave lifted us to the level of *Baquedano*'s deck. This was far from being the best and safest method of rescue, but it was the only one which had any prospect of success.

We slowly approached the grey hull with its two decks. I could not help being a little uneasy as to what would happen to us if the raft was crushed against the ship's side, but I quickly dismissed the unpleasant idea from my mind. My next worry was Eric, who was now so weak that I was not at all sure that he could manage the acrobatic feat which boarding the cruiser involved. Michel and I, therefore, kept close to him so as to be at hand if he should require any help. But before we could agree as to how we could best help him we had reached *Baquedano,* and a few minutes later, as if by request, we were shot up into the air as quickly as if in a lift. I suddenly saw just in front of me a long row of sailors with outstretched hands. At least half a dozen hands caught hold of Eric and dragged him on board. Much relieved, I took a flying leap and was caught by other helping hands.

While I was still looking round cautiously to see if any of us were missing—which thank heaven was not the case—I heard an ominous crashing behind me. I dashed to the rail. It was of course *Tahiti Nui* which had run into *Baquedano.* With the whole of her starboard side smashed in by the violent collision, the raft slid down at an angle into the trough of a wave and the whole deck went under water. There was a succession of sharp cracks as one mooring rope after another snapped. But when the sailors hauled in the ropes it appeared that one of them was still intact, and that it was one of the wooden Polynesian images, used by us as a bollard, that had broken loose. I took it carefully in my arms and patted it affectionately as a dear old friend.

I had hardly drawn a sigh of relief at our all having been saved when I was struck by a fearful thought. If the raft sank, what would happen to the poor *nanue* fish which had followed us so faithfully all the way from Tahiti? They were lagoon fish, and without any raft to hide themselves in they could easily be the victims of voracious predatory fish. Or they would go down into the depths with the raft and be crushed to death by the increased pressure. I looked out over the sea again. *Tahiti Nui* had already fallen far astern and had begun to sink, just as if she was tired and in despair at our cowardly flight and had suddenly lost all power of resistance. It was obviously too late to save the *nanue* fish. Besides, if I had rushed up on the bridge and asked the captain of *Baquedano* to launch a boat to save a few wretched fish, he would certainly have thought I was crazy and ignored my prayers. I stood at the rail, silent and all of a sudden curiously tired, and followed the rapidly sinking raft with moist eyes till she was out of sight.

Chapter 3

WE START ALL OVER AGAIN

When I woke next morning in my comfortable, tastefully furnished cabin on board *Baquedano,* after the best and deepest sleep of my life, I felt as relieved and lively as one who has at last regained his health after a serious illness. Clearly the last days on board the raft had been more tiring and more trying to the nerves than I had realized. Francis, whom I met in the alleyway, seemed as fit and well-rested as myself, but when we looked in on Eric to say good-morning, to our surprise we found him curled up dismally in a corner of his bunk. The crumpled sheets were a further indication that he had not slept very well.

'It's terribly hard to be obliged to give up so near the goal,' he said in a despairing voice. 'My having failed to prove my theory is bad enough. But of course by far the worst thing is that *Tahiti Nui* has been lost. It takes a long time to build a new raft—if I even manage to do so. But I've no right to complain if you're sick and tired of raft expeditions and would rather go home by boat or plane as soon as we get to Valparaiso. In other words, you are released from the promise you gave me before we left Tahiti to make the return voyage too.'

'Wait a minute, Eric,' said Francis eagerly. 'In the first place I don't agree with you at all that our expedition has been a failure. Our intention was to prove that it is possible to go on a bamboo raft from Polynesia to South America along a southerly route. But isn't that just what we have proved by our voyage of over 4000 miles? Surely no sane man can doubt that we should easily have covered the short distance on to Valparaiso if we had not had the extraordinary bad luck to meet the worst gale there has been in these waters for fifty years.'

'And in the second place,' I added with feeling and conviction, 'we're not in the least sick and tired of raft expeditions. We're all as determined as ever to go back to Tahiti with you on a new raft.'

Francis nodded agreement. Eric looked at us keenly and in silence for a long time, evidently uncertain whether we were serious or if we were only making a stupid and clumsy attempt to console him. At last a smile appeared on his lips, and he said curtly, with a new determination in his voice:

'Good, then we'll start again together.'

This seemed to decide the matter. At any rate we said no more about our new raft plans during the remainder of *Baquedano*'s two days' voyage to Valparaiso. This was accomplished in record time, and we arrived early in the afternoon of May 29. The first greeting from land we certainly found rather strange. It came from an aeroplane, which made straight for us as we glided into the harbour and dropped a large parcel attached to a parachute. Unluckily the parcel fell into the water several hundred yards from *Baquedano*. We gesticulated wildly to the passengers in a large motor-boat to get them to pick up our parcel. Instead of doing this the motor-boat steered straight for *Baquedano*, and before we could explain more clearly what we wanted the passengers jumped on to the gangway, which had just been lowered, and streamed on board. Next moment we were surrounded by a babbling crowd of men and women armed with notepads or cameras. I did not at once realize that they were journalists and photographers, and when I did my first instinct was to run away and hide. The only one of us who understood anything of the torrent of questions in Spanish was Juanito, and he, like the rest of us, was so taken aback by all the unaccustomed crowd and excitement that he could not utter a syllable. Our interviewers were visibly annoyed at finding us so tongue-tied and became still more aggressive.

Just at this critical moment we were fortunately rescued by our friend the secretary of the expedition, Carlos Garcia-Palacios, who also had come out in the motor-boat with the French Consul. With his help Carlos swept the whole crowd of pressmen into the saloon and began to interpret for us.

When the cross-examination was over at last Michel

drew a long breath and said faintly: 'That was the worst strain I've ever been through.'

'A good thing the excitement's all over, so that at any rate we can go ashore now and look round in peace and quiet,' I added.

For some reason Carlos grinned broadly at my remark. While I was still wondering why he thought it so funny, the Chilean naval commandant's own launch arrived to take us off. We felt far from worthy of this honour, especially as we looked incredibly shabby in our unpressed, fusty clothes alongside the imposing, well-dressed officers in the launch: but we jumped down into her all the same, eager to get ashore.

The quay seen at a distance seemed unusually high and uneven. When we came nearer we saw that this was because it was linked with several close-packed rows of people. I gazed at the huge crowd in curiosity and surprise, and thousands of pairs of eyes gazed back at me and my comrades. But not till we came alongside, and thousands of voices began to shout '*Viva la Tahiti Nui! Viva Francia!*' did I realize that they had all come together to greet us. As soon as we stepped ashore a large military band struck up the *Marseillaise*, after which the multitude closed about us, and we were slowly dragged by the cheering, laughing, yelling crowd towards a handsome building with a large balcony, which was Valparaiso town hall.

A couple of men in uniform helped us in through the door and double-locked it behind us. When we went out on to the balcony, where an official reception committee, headed by the mayor, was waiting for us, the square was black with enthusiastic people, and I could not help feeling relieved at being out of their reach. We waved back cheerfully, but curiously enough the crowd did not seem really satisfied. Soon the general noise gave place to one regular, incessantly repeated shout. Much puzzled, we listened attentively. There was no doubt about it. Our admirers were calling, more and more stubbornly and fiercely, for Juanito. It was only natural that Juanito's countrymen should wish to do honour to him in particular. But why were the cries so impatient and insistent? We looked questioningly at our Chilean comrade, and almost simultaneously we realized the position. Juanito, certainly not more than five feet tall, was completely hidden by the high balustrade, and—a poor compliment to us—his over-enthusiastic countrymen down in the square had certainly concluded that we had forgotten him. We hastened to lift him up on to our shoulders. A terrific shout hailed Juanito's belated appearance, and the remainder of the reception ceremony was completely drowned by the roars of applause, rising and falling like waves, from the square below.

More exhausted than we had been after any of the numerous storms we had encountered during our long voyage on the raft, we succeeded at last in reaching the hotel where Carlos had reserved rooms for us. Here a new surprise awaited us in a form of a soaking wet parcel addressed to Juanito. It was of course the same parcel which the pilot of the aeroplane had dropped into the water when we were arriving on board *Baquedano,* and it contained a warm overcoat, a particularly welcome gift, for it was already late autumn and the air was quite chilly. Who the kind donor was Juanito never found out, for he had left neither name nor address, and he never made himself known.

Next day we had another proof of the Chileans' extraordinary friendliness and interest in the expedition when the president of the largest yacht club in Chile called at the hotel and offered to help us in every imaginable way if we would only do them the honour of building our new raft in the club's yard in the neighbouring port of Quintero. Everything seemed to be turning out better than we had dared to hope in our wildest dreams. In the highest spirits we crowded into a couple of taxis and drove up to Santiago, the capital, to obtain building material and equipment for our return to the South Seas in, we believed, the near future.

But hardly had we begun to play in earnest the part, unusual for us, of popular heroes when we encountered a series of misadventures which suddenly brought our plans to nothing. The first thing was that Eric suddenly developed a very high temperature and had to be taken to hospital, where it was found that he had double pneumonia. Even when the doctors had gradually got the better of this, Eric's general condition was still so bad that they ordered absolute rest for at least a couple of months. Eric's illness and convalescence led to new and unforeseen difficulties. Our intention had been to build an exact copy of our first raft, so our first need was a thousand bamboos. As the bamboo is a tropical bush, which does not grow in the cool climate of Chile, we had intended to order the bamboos from Peru or Ecuador. Of course this would cost a lot of money, which Eric had promised to obtain by writing articles for one or two American and French illustrated papers. When, a few weeks later, Eric was well enough to write these articles, the papers which had commissioned them were no longer interested. So there we were with no money and no raft.

Eric, as usual, was completely unmoved. He assured us that he would soon earn several times the sum required from the book which a French publishing firm had commissioned him to write a long time before. We did not doubt for a moment that he would be able to write a readable and saleable book, but how long would it take? To tell the truth, on this point we were all a good deal more pessimistic and impatient than Eric himself. Michel in particular expressed his dissatisfaction in unnecessarily sharp language, which brought a number of old grievances to life again. The primary reason why Michel had found it harder to get on with Eric than the rest of us was that they had incompatible characters. Further, Michel held a master's certificate, too, and therefore had sometimes considered himself entitled to give Eric advice about navigation. But two captains on board one craft are one captain too many. Finally, if I mention that Michel had been married just after we left Tahiti, and that he had long been tired of being on his honeymoon alone, his impatience will at once become more understandable. At all events, none of us other members of the expedition were particularly surprised or indignant when he returned to Tahiti by air a few weeks after our arrival in Chile.

Immediately afterwards, Juanito went home to his mother at Puerto Montt, an isolated fishing port far down towards Cape Horn. It was quite natural that he should leave us, for strictly speaking he had only been a passenger with a single ticket, who had preferred to take a rather unusual route of return to his own country. Indeed, up to the last moment he talked of continuing the journey with us, but I was convinced that sooner or later we should be obliged to find a substitute for him too. Still, despite all our reverses, I never doubted for a moment that everything would come right in the end. I suppose it was the long voyage on board *Tahiti Nui* which had given me this firm confidence and optimistic faith, for one of the most conspicuous lessons we had learnt on it was that not even the most violent contrary wind lasts for ever.

As there was nothing for us to do but wait for a turn of fortune, at the beginning of July Francis and I accepted an invitation to see the shipyard at Constitucion, a small provincial town of about 4000 inhabitants, which lies 125 miles south of Santiago at the point where the river Maule runs out into the Pacific. To our surprise the owners of the eight shipyards not only showed us in detail how a type of cutter, which was their speciality, was built, but invited us to a big dinner at which many speeches were made and toasts were drunk in splendid wine from a neighbouring vineyard. Our Spanish was still very poor and the wine was very strong, so it was a

Almost hidden by all the sweet-scented flower wreaths which his friends and admirers had hung about him in Tahitian fashion, Eric de Bisschop bade a specially warm farewell to Bengt Danielsson when sailing from Tahiti on November 8, 1956.

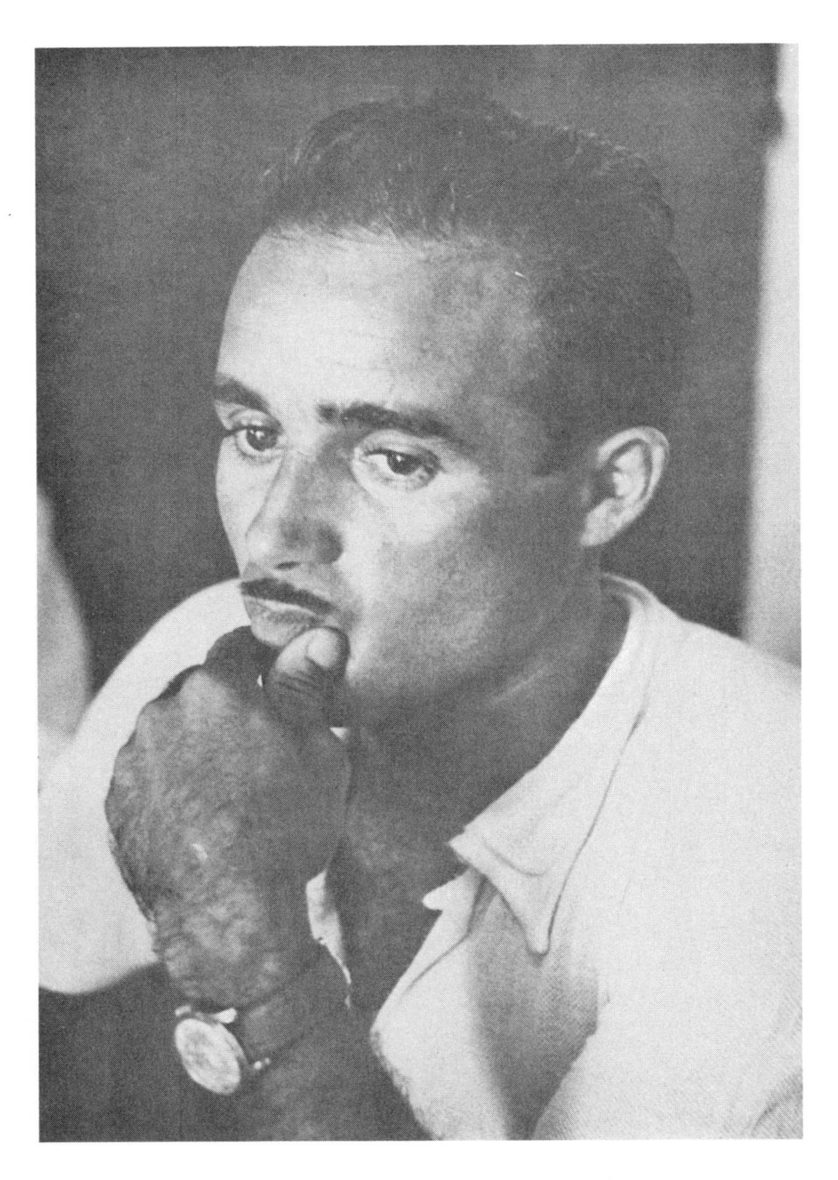

It was evident that Alain Brun was tormented by unpleasant memories, and it was a long time before he could bring himself to tell the true story of what had happened on the two tragic expeditions.

With her Chinese rig and her Peruvian centerboards, the bamboo raft *Tahiti Nui I,* which Eric de Bisschop and his comrades used for the voyage from Tahiti to Chile, was one of the most peculiar crafts ever built.

The bamboo raft *Tahiti Nui I,* gaily decorated from bow to stern, was towed out of Papeete harbor on November 8, 1956, and left to her fate about ten miles south of Tahiti.

Down in a latitude of 35° South, fishing was bad, and only on rare occasions could the cook offer such a delicacy as fillets of dolphin or tunny. To the left, Eric de Bisschop and Alain Brun.

Tahiti Nui I had lost quantities of worm-eaten bamboos and had a heavy list when the Chilean warship at last arrived and after several unsuccessful attempts finally took her in tow.

Like her predecessor, *Tahiti Nui II* had a raised deck, but she was built of cypress logs instead of bamboos. Contrary to all predictions, she floated well when she was launched.

Eric de Bisschop, surrounded by his companions, on board the raft immediately before sailing from Constitución on February 15, 1958.

Tahiti Nui II was towed out to sea by a string of rowing boats, after which the crew had to set sail quickly so that the raft should not drift back into the surf on the shore.

After forty-one days of pleasant sailing along the west coast of South America, *Tahiti Nui II* arrived according to program at Callao, where a tug immediately took her in tow.

Unmoved by all that went on round about him, Eric de Bisschop, as long as he was in good health, worked vigorously at the scientific thesis which he hoped would prove his revolutionary theories to be correct.

Alain Brun was the only man on board who was a seaman by profession, so that he had greater responsibility and more work than the other members of the crew.

Eric de Bisschop's companions. In front (left to right): Alain Brun (French) and Juanito Bugueño (Chilean). Behind: Hans Fischer (German-Chilean) and Jean Pélissier (French).

long time before we grasped the main point of all the speeches—that our kind hosts wanted to make us a present of a cutter. We also discovered by degrees that their generosity was to some extent dictated by a hope that orders for similar cutters would stream in from the South Sea islands as soon as we had made their excellent qualities known there—but this did not make their offer any less attractive to us. Elated by the Chilean wine and the pleasant prospect of becoming shipowners, we returned to Santiago to await the next offer of this kind. But when we told Eric what had happened he was not best pleased and said at once impatiently:

'But what do you want a boat for? Why didn't you ask for a raft instead?'

Although we felt very sad at having to give up our fine ship-owning plans so soon, we could not help admitting that Eric was right. After all, our stay in Chile was only an accidental break in our long raft voyage, and the most important thing at the moment was to get on as quickly as possible. We owed it to Eric that we had made this raft voyage to Chile and had been invited to Constitucion. So it was our definite duty to think first of Eric and the expedition. We wrote to the shipbuilders and explained the situation, and they sent Eric by return of post an invitation to come and see them.

Eric went off to Constitucion fitter, more self-confident and full of charm than he had been for a long time, while Francis and I remained in the capital and celebrated the coming victory in advance, for we knew that Eric was irresistible when he was in this humour. Indeed, he returned several days later and triumphantly declared that he had not had the least difficulty in persuading the shipbuilders to build a raft for us. Of course the building of the raft would not cost us one peso, and to judge from Eric's enthusiastic accounts it seemed that the whole population of the town had promised to come out and help us with our preparations quite free of charge. It was by no means as unlikely as it sounded, for by this time we knew both Eric and the Chileans very well.

The future looked bright again. But just as we were about to return to Constitucion to start building the raft Francis had a letter from Tahiti containing bad news. His wife was ill and must have an operation, and all his relations entreated him to come home. Francis decided with a heavy heart to fly back to Tahiti at once with our unwearying expedition secretary Carlos, who, having straightened things out for us in Chile, was now again hurrying on ahead to make preparations for our return. I saw the last of my raft-mates disappear with grief and a real sense of loss, and I felt depressed for the first time since we arrived in Chile. But fortunately Eric's energy and confidence were not affected in the slightest degree.

'So there's only you and me left,' he said in a matter of fact way. 'Let's divide the work between us. I've my book to think of, so you'll have to build the raft. That is to say, it'll really be enough for you to supervise the construction, for the builders are providing both labour and material. If it was possible I wouldn't mind exchanging with you, for the job is so infinitely easier and more interesting than mine.'

I was far from convinced that the simplest job had fallen to me, but I accepted this division of work as being the only possible one. Besides, I had always Eric to fall back upon for instructions and advice. Our first problem was to decide what kind of wood we should use for building the raft. Our friends the shipbuilders had given Eric a collection of samples of wood, which we now produced. To make our raft of balsa, as the *Kon-Tiki* men did, was out of the question, for no balsa trees grew in Chile and we had neither time nor money to send to Ecuador for the quite considerable quantity of timber that would be needed.

After we had shown our samples to innumerable timber merchants and shipbuilders we began, as the majority of them did, to incline to the view that cypress wood would be the most suitable. Several people objected that cypress wood was only used for coffins, and we should therefore do best to avoid it. But, as we soon discovered, this assertion was wrong, for many boats were made of this kind of wood. The fact that it was also used for coffins naturally made no difference one way or the other, unless one had an unusually grisly imagination. To be on the safe side we decided to postpone our final choice till we had heard what the builders at Constitucion thought. So, as soon as we arrived there—on September 8, 1957—we laid our problem before them. One of them immediately lifted up his voice and said:

'*Muy estimados señores*. The only raft we have built here was an oak raft, which the Government ordered a few years ago to carry cars to and fro across the Maule a little higher up, where there is no bridge. She was a fine large raft, *señores,* and several ministers, provincial governors, mayors and a lot of other fine people had been invited to the launching. A band of fifty played military music and a lot of speeches were made. Finally came the solemn moment when the raft was to be committed to her right element. She glided down the slip at a good pace, plunged into the water—and began to sink fast! A few minutes later only a few light ripples on the surface showed where the handsome, expensive raft rested on the river bottom. She was too heavy to be raised, and possibly she is still lying where she sank. That is all the experience we have of rafts, *señores*. As for cypress wood, it is just the kind of wood we use for building the cutters which have made Constitucion famous, and no better cutters are built anywhere in the world, I'm convinced of that.'

This decided the matter. Cypress was quite certainly the right kind of wood for us too. Another advantage was that there were large cypress forests quite close to the town. Eric and I went for a walk in the woods with Don Enrique Muñoz, in whose yard our raft was to be built, and chose some fifty trunks about eighteen inches thick. As soon as Don Enrique had marked them, he set a gang at work felling them at once.

'I'm glad the building is in such good hands,' Eric said with satisfaction on our return to the hotel and began to collect his few belongings. 'As I can't do anything more here I'm going to Lontue, where some Chilean friends have promised to put me up. It's a pretty hacienda high up in the mountains, and is certainly an ideal place to finish my book in peace and quiet. So good luck—'

'But wait a bit, Eric,' I interrupted him. 'You haven't given me any sketch for the raft.'

Eric looked perfectly astonished.

'What do you want a sketch for? You ought to know quite well by this time what a raft looks like. Make as faithful a copy as you can of *Tahiti Nui I*. The most important thing is that she shall have the same measurements. Well, good luck. I must be off now.'

In the next moment he had disappeared.

I remembered quite well how we had set about the building of our bamboo raft in the naval yard at Papeete, but unfortunately this dearly bought experience was of little use to me, for this time the problems were different because the material we were using was different. For example, it was impossible to lash the thick cypress trunks together by the same simple and quick method which we had employed for our first raft. After puzzling my head over this for a long time I decided not to use any ropes at all, fearing that they would be chafed to pieces by the hard, rough trunks, and adopted instead the ancient system of wooden pegs. Each layer of trunks—there were three in all—was kept together by wooden pegs of harder timber, which were driven in from the side slantwise right through all the trunks. The three layers were then joined together in the same way with similar pegs inserted vertically. In constructing the raised deck, cabin and masts it was easier to copy the prototype, and I made only one alteration—a small but very fortunate one, as was seen later: I gave the cabin a flat roof instead of a sloping one. As a mascot, and a reminder that despite all changes our goal was still the same, I fixed the Polynesian image, which we had so luckily saved at the last moment from *Tahiti Nui I,* immediately behind the centreboard in the stern of the new raft.

Now and then Eric came down from his mountain retreat, nodded approvingly, said a few friendly words and disappeared as quickly as he had come. On another occasion a young Frenchman whose acquaintance we had made in Santiago turned up and declared that Eric had just taken him on as a member of our expedition. Jean Pélissier, as my new comrade was called, was unusually well qualified for a voyage of the kind we meant to undertake, for he was an oceanographer by profession. He had taken part in several Arctic expeditions while a student at the Geophysical Institute at Bergen in Norway: he had then obtained a post at the marine biological station in Chile and had done research work both in the Antarctic and in the waters round Easter Island. I was therefore convinced that he was a man of the right type, with plenty of hardiness and endurance, which on a long sea voyage is at least as important as the possession of theoretical knowledge, however valuable.

Jean mentioned that he had a Chilean friend, a mining engineer with the un-Chilean name of Hans Fischer, who seemed to have a good chance of also being taken on by Eric. Unfortunately neither Jean nor Hans could come and help me with the building of the raft till the

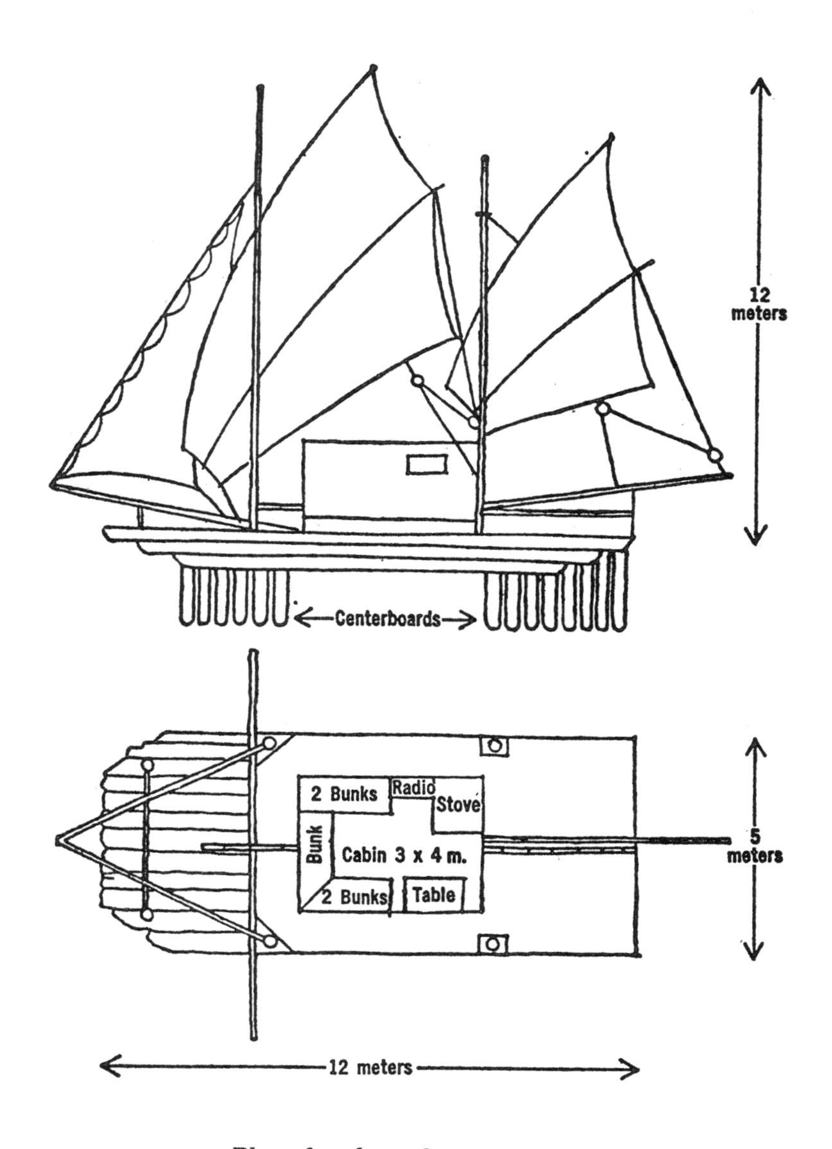

Plan of timber raft TAHITI NUI II
built for the voyage from Chile to Polynesia

end of the year at the earliest, because they had first to complete some important scientific research work.

I was rather annoyed at seeing Jean disappear so quickly, for I really needed all the help I could get if I was to have the raft ready in time for us to complete our voyage before the cyclone season began in the South Sea islands. Immediately afterwards, however, I received the support I needed from another quite unexpected quarter when Juanito arrived with a cheerful grin on his face and immediately began to make himself useful in his usual considerate way. I was by no means sure that the authorities in Tahiti would be any more tender-hearted this time, but I dared not destroy his beautiful dreams. It made a great difference to have a comrade who was a Chilean by birth and not only spoke Spanish fluently but also knew how to handle his countrymen, and from that moment the tempo of the work increased considerably.

But the work would certainly have gone still more quickly if we had not been so popular. From the first moment the good people of Constitucion had shown an extraordinary interest in our raft-building, and as strictly speaking they were all our hosts, and many of them had helped us in different ways, it would have been both rude and foolish to turn them away. So although we sometimes felt like queer animals in a zoological garden, we reconciled ourselves to being continually stared at. But as time passed our crowd of spectators increased in numbers and at the same time became more demanding and difficult to manage. As I soon found out, this unwelcome change was due mainly to the fact that it was gradually getting warmer. Constitucion was a very popular watering-place, visited every summer by thousands of holiday-makers from Santiago and Valparaiso, and in that particular summer they seemed to be unusually numerous and frolicsome.

As long as they contented themselves with a good joke we did not mind, but many of them regarded our enterprise simply as a bad joke, a very bad joke indeed. After I had answered, several hundred times a day over a long period, such silly questions as whether we really thought the raft would float, whether we were going to Tahiti or Haiti, and why we did not build a boat instead, I almost wanted to put up a notice such as Eric had nailed to a tree when he was building his remarkable double canoe *Kaimiloa* in Honolulu in 1936. It read simply: 'WE KNOW WE ARE CRAZY, SO PLEASE DON'T TRY TO PROVE IT TO US!' But I had not Eric's gift of ruthless irony, and many of our well-meaning benefactors would certainly have been quite unnecessarily hurt.

A visitor whom we always greeted with pleasure was the stationmaster of Constitucion, Horacio Blanco. Blanco was a most unusual combination of a dynamic man of action and an unselfish idealist. We gradually learnt that it was originally he who had persuaded the owners of the shipyards to take an interest in our expedition and make us their generous offer. Blanco's sole motive was his strong patriotism, or perhaps I ought to say local patriotism: he wanted to restore to Constitucion the greatness and importance it had possessed in the sixteenth and seventeenth centuries, when ships from its harbour made regular long voyages to Panama and Europe. It was, by the way, the town's greatest son, Juan Fernandez, who on one of his many adventurous voyages discovered the islands that now bear his name.

Horacio Blanco was firmly convinced that the building of the raft would not only be the opening of a new and glorious epoch in the town's history, but would also stimulate its flagging business life. As he only had four trains a day to deal with he was able to devote most of his time to helping us, and he seemed to possess a kind of sixth sense when it was a question of guessing our wishes and needs and finding out the best way of satisfying them. If by any chance on some rare occasion he had not time to come himself, he sent us instead some of his eleven children, all of whom seemed to have inherited their father's energy and inventiveness.

Indeed, as time passed I became so accustomed to the idea that Blanco could arrange anything and everything that I took it as the most natural thing in the world that he should initiate me into the mysteries of the Morse code—Eric having on one of his occasional visits appointed me, to my astonishment, not only second in command but also wireless operator to the expedition. After that I began my working day an hour earlier with lessons in Morse at Constitucion station, which fortunately was only a few hundred yards from the slip.

Blanco also undertook—without, as far as I can remember, anyone asking him to do so—to obtain provisions, medical stores, sails, anchors and all the rest of the equipment which we needed for our voyage of at least five months. How he managed it I have no idea, but anyhow towards Christmas large cases began to arrive in a steady stream from different shops and factories, and the only thing we had to do was to say thank you and receive them. I think I can say in all seriousness that without Blanco's selfless assistance the building of the raft and preparations for our return voyage would have taken twice as long and cost a great deal of money.

At the beginning of January 1958, Eric arrived—as usual, without warning—and told me with a grin of satisfaction that he had almost finished his book. He assured me with delight that it was a very malicious book, which would certainly annoy a lot of people.[1] I told him, not without some pride, that Juanito and I too had nearly finished our task. The raft had been ready for launching for a long time, and the work which remained to be done was mainly on cabin fittings. We promised to finish them in good time if he would only let us know when we were to sail.

'The Santiago papers say we are to sail on February 15th,' Eric replied with an ironical smile. 'I've no idea who spread this baseless rumour. But let's help the papers to be right for once in a way by making this our sailing date.'

[1] Unfortunately, it appeared later that he was right on this point. This book, recently published in Great Britain under the title *Tahiti Nui*, is also somewhat marred by serious inaccuracies and omissions, understandable if we keep in mind the conditions in which it was written.

Of course, neither Juanito nor I had any objection to offer.

As a rule, every new ship has a trial trip before she starts on a real voyage, and when we built our first raft we had adhered to this sensible custom. This time, unfortunately, we could not have any trial trips on account of the peculiar conditions in the port of Constitucion—a serious disadvantage, of which we had not been aware when we decided to build the raft there. The main obstacle was that the shipyard where we had built the raft, and all the other shipyards, lay on the bank of the broad and swift Maule river about three-quarters of a mile from its mouth. In the course of centuries the river had carried down huge quantities of sand and gravel, which had gradually formed a broad underwater barrier right across the mouth of the river. The river water streaming out and the heavy swell from the Pacific met at this barrier, which in places rose almost to the surface, and formed an unbroken line of foaming breakers. Just to get out through this infernal barrier was a risky business: to return through it against the stream was impossible. This was why we had at an early stage given up all idea of making a trial trip. Or, more correctly, Eric had solved the problem in his usual grand manner with this brief announcement:

'Let us regard the first stage of the voyage, from here to Callao, as a trial trip. It will certainly be rather a long trial trip, for it is 1500 miles from Constitucion to Callao, but this is in a way an advantage, for we shall get to know the qualities of the raft much more thoroughly than if we had pottered about in the sea off Constitucion for a few days.'

We had agreed with Eric as usual.

About a week after Eric's lightning visit Jean and his friend Hans Fischer (whom Eric had just taken on as a member of the expedition) arrived with a whole lorry-load of oceanographical and meteorological equipment. My new comrade did not look at all like a Chilean, for he was fair and blue-eyed and had a ruddy complexion, so I was not in the least surprised when I heard that his parents were immigrants from Germany. Hans was extremely good-natured and pleasant, but fearfully unpractical, and what was worse an absolute landlubber, so I was anything but delighted at Eric's choice. While I was still racking my brains over the apparently insoluble problem of where I was to find room on board the raft for all these queer instruments and apparatus, Jean dashed back to Santiago—to fetch more gear!

We finished the last jobs a good week before the launching, which was fixed for February 12th. Everything else seemed to be according to time-table—with two exceptions. Jean was still away in Santiago, and as if it had not been enough to be one man short, Juanito suddenly disappeared. Eric, who had now come to live at Constitucion, seemed for once seriously worried: I never quite understood why, for there were hundreds of highly qualified people begging and praying to be allowed to come with our expedition. But only a few days later Juanito returned, utterly exhausted and with an expression of beatitude on his face suggesting that he had been paying a particularly thorough adieu to the delights of life ashore. Also, he had somehow acquired a fixed idea: he absolutely refused to continue to be cook to the expedition. So Eric had the bright idea of appointing him superintendent of food supplies, a position which the unsuspecting Juanito accepted with gratitude. Hard on Juanito's heels Jean at last arrived with ten cases of empty bottles which he intended to fill with water and samples of plankton during the voyage. He declared with a grave face that he was a trifle late simply because it had been so difficult to find corks for the bottles. I almost believed him.

The launching took place, as was right and proper, under Horacio Blanco's supervision, and all the inhabitants of Constitucion and all the summer visitors seemed to have come to witness the remarkable event. Most ot them had evidently expected the worst, for when our imposing raft slid gracefully out on to the river, a cry of astonishment rose from a thousand throats to the blue summer sky: 'She floats, she floats!' The raft did not exactly float like a cork, but she sank no deeper than the third and last layer of trunks, and the deck was a good eighteen inches above the surface of the water. We were busy for the rest of that day and most of the following day embarking all our equipment and provisions, so that it was not till late in the afternoon of February 14th that we were able to summon the motor boat which was to tow us to a small harbour called La Poza, at the mouth of the river.

Before we could stop them about fifty of our keenest

supporters had jumped on board. As this was an excellent way of submitting the raft to a final test of endurance, we let them stay, and were glad to observe that despite this heavy load the raft sank only an inch or two deeper. We moored her to the concrete wharf at La Poza in an unusually optimistic frame of mind and directed our steps to one of the numerous restaurants in the town, where the owners of the shipyards had arranged a farewell dinner in our honour. Horacio Blanco alone was missing; unselfish and helpful as ever, he had preferred to remain on board the raft to look after her and to fill our six forty-gallon water drums with drinking water.

When, at dawn on February 15th, we returned to La Poza from our most delightful farewell party, Blanco was still fiddling about with his water-hoses and looked worried. He told us that unluckily there had been a leak somewhere in the town's water system, and that in consequence he had only been able to fill two of the six tanks. With his usual resourcefulness he proposed that we should ring up the fire brigade and ask for help, for even if the town was otherwise dry—which, it seemed, did happen sometimes—there ought always to be some filled hoses or reserve supplies at the fire station. We took his good advice, but the only result of our call was a sleepy voice that told us that the chief of the fire brigade had just gone off to La Poza with all his men to see if those crazy Frenchmen would get through the breakers with their clumsy raft. But if we rang up again in the afternoon, the telephone operator added, we would certainly get as much water as we liked. We thanked him heartily for his kind offer and hurriedly agreed that 100 gallons of water would be ample for the six or seven weeks we reckoned the voyage up the coast to Callao would take.

The first spectators had arrived even before we did, and only half an hour later their numbers had increased so greatly that we were obliged to take refuge on board the raft to get a little elbowroom. But it was not long before the raft too was full of excited Chileans, who eagerly crowded round us to wish us *buen viaje,* shake hands with us, give us flowers, embrace us, kiss us and ask for our autographs. Many of our well-wishers, curiously enough, gave us their own autographs in exchange—a queer custom initiated several months previously at the shipyard by a boy who had once written his name on the cabin wall. Although we tried hard to stop it, it soon became quite usual for our visitors to treat the raft as an autograph book. I had thought that the book had been full for a long time, but I soon saw that I had been quite mistaken, for throughout the farewell ceremony we were continually stumbling over squatting figures inscribing their names on the cypress trunks or cabin walls.

Despite the fearful crowd and the deafening noise we did our best to keep in touch with our guests of honour, who included, besides the incomparable Horacio Blanco and all the prominent people of the province, the French Ambassador to Chile and his teenage daughter. As a mark of gratitude for their kindness in making the long journey from Santiago just on our account, we invited these two to accompany us a little way out to sea, and to our surprise they accepted without a moment's hesitation. Immediately afterwards our halting conversation was brutally interrupted by the two largest bands in the province, each of them more than fifty men strong, which together struck up first the Chilean national anthem and then the *Marseillaise.*

Whether by agreement or not, at the same moment our tugs appeared—five open rowing boats, each manned by four or six sturdy fellows. As Horacio Blanco had assured us that rowing boats of this kind were used whenever a cutter had to be towed through the river barrier, we made fast the ropes flung over to us without protest although this method of towing did seem to us a little primitive. As though reading our thoughts, the rowers explained that a cutter would take over the towing as soon as we got out into deep water, and that if we wished she could stand by the raft till we were sure that we could manage by ourselves. This information reassured us at once.

A quarter of an hour later a cutter came along the coast before the wind and lay to outside the breakers which she had cleared without mishap a few hours earlier. At a sign from the commander of the teams of rowers we quickly cast off our moorings and slid away from the quay, while the thousands of spectators waved miniature Chilean and French flags, and cheered till the hills echoed. We had plenty of time to wave back, for our rowers rested on their oars as soon as they were a hundred yards from the quay and remained motionless with their faces turned towards the breakers which barred the way. We found it hard to wait as quietly and silently as they did, so much more was at stake. Our patience was nearly at an end when the men in the rowing boats suddenly grasped their oars, dipped them in the water and began to row with all their might. The raft, pitching and lurching, reluctantly approached the huge foaming breakers.

'She can never do it,' I heard someone mutter behind my back, when a few seconds later a gigantic wave towered up in front of us.

But just when we seemed to be plunging right into the giant wave it sank as quickly and unexpectedly as it had risen, and we were sliding at top speed into a deep valley. The raft, rocking unsteadily, at last climbed slowly up again and checked herself abruptly. I looked quickly round me and heaved a sigh of relief. The breakers were astern.

To our surprise, a fresh southerly wind was blowing, a fact of which we had been in happy ignorance because the quay at La Poza was under the shelter of a high rock. The raft, with her large cabin, naturally caught the wind much more than the small rowing boats, and it was not long before we were towing our tugs. To make matters even worse, the wind was driving us back rapidly towards the breakers. We looked eagerly for the cutter which according to plan was to take over the towing as soon as we were out into open water. She was not far off, but for some reason she was going away instead of approaching. So as not to drag any innocent persons to destruction along with ourselves, we quickly cut the entangled tow-ropes which connected us with the rowing boats. They fled from the breakers in every direction like unleashed dogs, while we ourselves continued to drift inexorably towards them.

As we had counted on being able to hoist the sails and put in the centreboards in peace and quiet far out to sea, we had not yet agreed as to how the different manoeuvres should be carried out. For that matter we did not even know whether the sails and centreboards worked as they should. But clearly we had none to rely on in this critical situation but ourselves, so Eric did the only possible thing: he sprang up on to a packing-case and began to bellow orders like the toughest privateer captain. To tell the truth, the ambassador knew much more about sailing and was much quicker in his movements than either of the new arrivals, Jean and Hans, and I really do not know how we should have fared without this admirable extra hand. As it was we got the sails up and the centreboards down just before we reached the breakers, and after a few anxious seconds, to our indescribable relief the raft swung slowly round and moved slowly away.

When soon afterwards a motor-boat came out to take off our gallant ambassador and his daughter we were already far out of the danger zone. The wind had freshened considerably, and we hoisted one or two more sails, joking and laughing, and steered straight out to sea, firmly convinced that the worst part of the voyage was over.

Chapter 4

ALL WELL ON BOARD

A glance at the chart suggests that it is the simplest thing in the world to sail up along the west coast of South America from Chile to Peru, for southerly winds predominate and the strong Humboldt Current helps the ship along. From whatever point along the Chilean coast a vessel puts to sea, she inevitably gets a set northward. Eric, however, apparently contrary to all reason, had decided long before our departure that we should cross the Humboldt Current at once and follow the coast at a distance of about 200 miles till we were approaching Callao.

His reasons for this unexpected decision were four in number. In the first place, the current was in places so strong and capricious that a sailing vessel like ours, without a motor, might easily become impossible to steer. In the second, adverse winds often sprang up along the coast, and head winds we must avoid at all costs, since we could not beat up against them. Thirdly, there were dangerous whirlpools just north of Valparaiso which it would be safest to avoid. Fourthly and last, there was busy shipping traffic in the middle of the Humboldt Current, and Eric knew from dearly bought experience that large passenger ships and freighters seldom notice small, badly-lighted craft and therefore do not keep out of their way.

For these reasons, which on closer consideration were very easy to understand, we steered right out to sea as soon as we were alone. Although it was full summer the wind was bitterly cold, the sky quite covered by black clouds and the sea so disturbed that the raft rolled and lurched violently, which had a devastating effect on the two newcomers' morale and appetite. Eric, Juanito and I, as the hardened old salts we were, thoroughly enjoyed the freedom and the quiet from the very first and quickly resumed our old habits from *Tahiti Nui I*. Eric in particular adapted himself with amazing ease: he simply hung up his briefcase on a nail over his bunk and took out his beloved papers and books: then he felt at home at once. This matchless power of adapting himself was of course due mainly to the fact that he lived entirely in a private world of his own and seldom noticed where he was and what was going on round him.

To my great delight the raft showed herself to be an excellent sea boat and almost steered herself. This made it an absolute pleasure to take a watch, for all one had to do was to sit down on the long bench which I had placed aft and keep an eye on the sails and the centreboards.

Thus even Jean and Hans could soon take their turns with the rest of us, but it was naturally some while before they were experienced enough to see in time when the raft was threatening to swing round and learnt how to prevent it.

Just a week after we sailed—immediately after we had passed the thirtieth degree of latitude—the sun broke through the clouds for the first time and began to thaw our frozen joints. At the same time, no doubt by pure chance, the rhythm of the waves became much quieter and more even. The spirits of the whole crew rose by several degrees, and both Jean and Hans at last got rid of their sea-sickness. Although they now had raging appetites after their long period of starvation, they had as much difficulty as the rest of us in swallowing the food which Juanito sulkily prepared. He had realized at last that his new post of 'superintendent of food supplies' bore an extraordinary resemblance to his old job as cook on board *Tahiti Nui I*. He took his revenge by providing scarcely anything but stale macaroni, half-cooked rice mixed with an enormous quantity of bitter onions and a kind of pancake which was regularly burnt on one side and sticky on the other. We were obliged to be very economical with our meagre supply of water, but luckily we had fifteen large demijohns of red wine which a kind Chilean lady had given us just before we sailed, and thanks to this we were able to wash down these peculiar and monotonous dishes. But not even Juanito could in the long run avoid being influenced by the lovely tropical sun which went on shining with undiminished strength, and at last he became the same tolerable cook and jolly shipmate which he had always been.

Similarly only a few days of sunshine were needed to liven Jean up sufficiently to make a start on his oceanographical researches. What interested him most was taking samples of water at different depths by means of a long line fitted with an ingenious gadget which shut the bottle before it was hauled up. By analysing these samples of water on our return it would, he declared, be possible to determine the direction and volume of the ocean currents. Eric, who had spend most of the sixty-eight years of his life in a successful study of the ocean currents with much simpler apparatus, could not help chaffing his colleague of twenty-five a little on his blind belief in the superiority of modern methods, and this wounded Jean deeply. The relations between the two men naturally became no better when, immediately afterwards, Jean quite innocently began to talk of his plan of capturing a giant squid and cutting off one of its tentacles. A well-known scientist had asked him to do this, he said, and he had even brought a special cask for the purpose. Eric, who was always as ironical at the expense of others as at his own, could not resist the temptation to make fun of this grotesque plan, in which Jean and Hans fully and firmly believed.

A week or two later Jean tried to take his revenge in an unusually silly and thoughtless manner. The sea, till then empty and desolate, suddenly began to teem with dolphins (a brilliantly coloured fish which must not be confused with the small, toothed whale, which is also called a dolphin). They were, as usual, extremely inquisitive and playful: time after time they swam swiftly up to the side of the raft and took a look at us, after which they turned about quickly and leapt high out of the water for sheer astonishment at the strange sight. Their impudence naturally made us keener to catch them, so I immediately set about making a harpoon. This I did by carefully fastening an iron pin to one end of a long stick with a strip of plaster from the medicine chest. I had often watched Francis and Michel harpooning fish with simple contrivances of this kind during our outward voyage, but I had never managed to attain any degree of skill. As neither Francis nor Michel was now on board I did my best to replace them, but however hard I tried I could not catch the tiniest dolphin. Nor were Eric's attempts to catch one on a hook baited with tinfoil any more successful. Jean watched us critically without saying anything, and waited till the next day before proceeding to action.

As soon as breakfast was over, while the rest of us were continuing our vain efforts, he suddenly came out of the cabin with a pair of swimming fins, a mask, a breathing-tube and a spear-gun in his hands. He pulled on his diving equipment at top speed and jumped into the water, while at the same moment Hans quickly flung a long rope over the side. Half a minute later Jean was bobbing about in our wake fifty yards astern of the raft, gripping the end of the rope firmly with one hand and holding the spear-gun at the ready in the other. This was a daring method of fishing, which we others had never tried. But why should we not let Jean try to fish in this way if he wanted to? We knew he was reputed to be an experienced frogman and a clever fisherman, and as long as he kept a tight hold of the rope the risk was very small—if there were no man-eating sharks about.

But suddenly, to our alarm, Jean let go of the end of the rope and dived. When at last he came to the surface again he was a good ten yards astern of the rope. The wind was unusually light on that day, so that his situation was still far from catastrophic. But instead of swimming quickly to grasp the end of the rope, as any sensible person would have done, Jean began to tread water and wave one of his arms. For a moment I really thought that he had been attacked by a shark, but then we saw that he had been brainless enough to take his booty, a large dolphin, in his arms, which of course hindered his movements.

Before I had been able to think out any means of saving him Hans plunged into the sea with a violent splash. Good heavens, I thought, what will happen to this clumsy lout who can't control his arms and legs even on dry land? (I am ashamed to say that I had not yet come to the point of intervening myself.) But Hans reached his comrade with astonishing speed, took the spear-gun from him and began to tow both fish and man by means of the line which was fastened to the arrow, which was fixed in the fish, which Jean held in his arms. After several anxious moments the pair reached the end of the rope, and of course we were not slow to haul them on board.

'I suppose you're proud of yourself now, you silly fool,' Eric shouted furiously as soon as Jean had crawled on board, still clasping the bleeding dolphin. 'But I wonder if you'd have been as well pleased if the raft had sailed away from you and you'd had to swim ashore! It's a nice little swim, 200 miles. As you don't seem to have grasped it, I must tell you that the raft can't stop or turn back. So everything that falls overboard, the crew included, is gone for good. And next time you want to show what a smart fisherman you are, for Heaven's sake don't take a bleeding fish in your arms like that. There's nothing whets a shark's appetite so much as blood, and if there had been any about it's not likely they'd have contented themselves with the dolphin.'

It was a long time before Eric's anger subsided. To pacify him a little I proposed that we should prepare a dish of raw fish in the Tahitian style. The proposal was at once received with general approval. Juanito cut up the dolphin into small lumps, and put these to soak for a couple of hours in the juice of a dozen lemons—an important necessity which luckily was included in our stores. As soon as the raw fish appeared on the table our depressed morale rose considerably, but from this incident, unfortunately, the relations between these two ill-matched men, who in fact had only one thing in common —their keen interest in oceanic studies—were never again as cordial as they had been. As Hans took his friend's side even more stoutly than before, the expedition even at this early stage was split into two, with poor bewildered Juanito forming a third, or neutral, party.

But to be just I will add at once that in the course of time Jean obtained a well-deserved rehabilitation. As both Eric and I and all the rest of us frankly admitted, he showed himself after this to be both a clever and a shrewd fisherman, without whose welcome contributions our fare would have been infinitely more monotonous. To the general satisfaction he also altered his method of fishing somewhat by tying a long fishing line tightly to the iron arrow of the spear-gun and entrusting the other end of this fishing line to Hans. As soon as Jean had shot the arrow into a fish Hans saw that the quarry was brought into safety while Jean himself was able to concentrate undisturbed on getting on board the raft again.

Both the radiantly beautiful summer weather and the fresh favourable wind continued, and each day we did longer and longer runs. When I marked our position on the chart on March 8th I was not greatly surprised to find that we were half-way already. Eight hundred miles in three weeks represented an average speed of forty miles a day, so we had certainly no cause for complaint.

But if the raft's sailing performance was above expectations, in another respect her behaviour was rather peculiar: her stern gradually sank deeper and deeper, and at last the waves were positively threatening to wash up on to the deck. It was not very probable that the same trunks should have absorbed more water aft than forward, so we decided that our heaviness astern was more likely due to the cargo being unevenly distributed, and to test this theory we moved forward all Jean's cases of sample bottles, hundreds of which were already full of salt water or plankton. This had an immediate effect, but not so much as we had hoped. The only cargo which now remained aft was four empty forty-gallon drums below decks. It suddenly occurred to us that salt water might have got into one or more of them. We examined them without delay. Two of the drums were indeed found to be full of sea water, so that they were weighing the raft down instead of increasing her buoyancy. With a good deal of trouble we at last succeeded in emptying them. The raft, freed from this enormous extra weight, immediately resumed her horizontal position. Perhaps she still lay a trifle deeper than when we left Constitucion: but of course it was only normal that the dry trunks should absorb a certain amount of water at the beginning of the voyage, and we were convinced that it was only a question of time when this process would end. For that matter, it seemed as if this stage had already been reached, for henceforward the raft floated lightly and well. So we ceased to worry about the matter.

I cannot remember now if it was because this little misadventure reminded us of our mortality, or if the cause was a sudden access of conscientiousness, but anyhow we now got out our wireless for the first time and tried to contact some of the fans in Chile who were sure to be listening eagerly. As on the outward voyage in *Tahiti Nui I,* we had two transmitters on board: a small one for telegraphy and a larger one for telephony. (We had also a simple receiver, which we seldom used.) The small one was driven by a battery, but the larger could only be worked by a petrol generator—an expensive thing which we could not afford to buy before sailing, but which we had good hopes of being able to get at Callao. During our voyage to that port the small transmitter ought to be sufficient for our needs: we had all agreed about that. I set up the aerial with inexperienced hands and sent out a call signal. The nice little apparatus seemed to be working as it should, but whatever the reason might be neither I nor Jean, who was my deputy as wireless operator, got any reply to our calls. We repeated the attempt for several days in succession without getting any sound whatever in reply.

None of us took this very seriously, for we were in no trouble, and to tell the truth we were almost glad to escape the veritable quiz programmes with which many fans had plagued us during our outward voyage in *Tahiti Nui I*. Moreover, we were now approaching the coast again. Or, to put it more correctly, the coast was approaching us, for immediately north of the frontier between Chile and Peru the South American continent projects in a wide bulge to westward. So without changing our course, which from the beginning of the voyage had been due north, we were now suddenly making for land again. We sighted the majestic mountain chain of the Andes, which runs parallel to the coast for its whole length from north to south, for the first time on March 20th, and were welcomed by a party of playful seals, which performed the most extraordinary circus tricks, evidently from sheer joy at seeing us. After standing a long way out to sea during the night for safety's sake, next day we continued to sail towards the coast and began to follow it northward at a distance of a few miles. This playing at being a coaster was by no means free from risk, but we had no choice if we were to avoid such an ignominious disaster as to miss Callao and drift out to sea again.

As we glided slowly onward along a steep stony beach, inside which a desolate sand desert stretched as far as we could see in every direction, Eric told us about the strange Nazca people, who far back in pre-Inca times had succeeded in cultivating the whole of this desert area by means of an ingenious system of irrigation. I tried to imagine how the Nazcas would have received strange sailors arriving from the South Sea islands on a raft, and lost myself in dreams which were not all of the most agreeable nature.

A short time afterwards I was brusquely recalled to modernity by Eric, who, with an ironical smile playing about the corners of his mouth, pointed out that the wind had died away and that we were drifting slowly towards the coast. I could do no more about it than Eric, for it had become quite impossible to steer the raft. Even if we had had oars or ship's boats it would not have helped us much, for it would have been useless to try to row or tow such a heavy raft. Accordingly we did the only possible thing: we sat down on the long bench aft and hoped for a miracle. The unwelcome calm had set in about 4 P.M. Not till 7 P.M., when we were so near the breakers on the beach that the noise of them drowned our excited talk, did the first breath of wind, miraculously indeed, come to us over the smooth surface. Fortunately enough, the wind, which rose quickly, was from the south-east, and we were not slow to remove ourselves from that inhospitable coast.

As we were now in waters where there was a good deal of traffic, Eric gave us strict orders to keep a good look-out, especially during the night watches. But no ships were sighted until the morning of March 24th, when we all perceived, practically at the same moment, a British cargo ship only a few miles away. Although we had kept a long way off the coast for the greater part of our voyage, we had already met five or six ships, and several of them had passed quite close. But none of them had detected us, which all things considered was not very surprising. A small low raft of a dirty grey colour blends extremely well with the marine landscape. We were therefore both astonished and flattered when the British ship quite unexpectedly sounded her siren and dipped her ensign, and we were not slow to answer her greeting. Only a few hours later a northward-bound Peruvian tanker overtook us. Presumably thinking, quite understandably, that we were shipwrecked, her captain steered right towards us. He stopped his engines about 300 yards from the raft. We could read the tanker's name, *Oyala,* quite plainly on her bow, and we saw with mixed feelings that two sailors aft were dragging a tow rope to the rail. With diminished speed *Oyala* continued to glide on through the water and finally lay across the bows of the raft. As we had a fair wind, we were far from pleased at the Peruvian captain's helpfulness. We gesticulated to him wildly, indicating that we wanted him to back, and shouted in three or four different languages that all was well on board and that we could take ourselves to Callao without difficulty. It was only after long hesitation that *Oyala*'s captain abandoned his plans for saving us and proceeded northward. Another ship passed shortly afterwards, but to our relief did not notice us.

That same evening we came into the dangerous waters off the famous prehistoric burial ground at Paracas, where according to the chart several strong currents met. We had no desire to end our days in this burial ground, however famous it might be, and therefore spent an uneasy sleepless night looking out for ships' lights, of which there were more than we liked, and a lighthouse which never appeared. (Presumably the Peruvian lighthouse keepers were on strike, as the French telegraphists had been when I arrived at the Marquesas Islands in *Kaumoana*.) When dawn came we were already, thank heaven, a good way off Paracas and had not suffered the slightest mishap. We were only eighty miles from Callao, and as both wind and current were with us two easy days' runs would take us there.

We were always eager to grasp at any imaginable excuse for having a bit of a party, so we got out one of our last bottles of Chilean brandy and sat down in the stern. While we were still sitting there, laughing and joking and drinking toasts, a red two-engined airplane suddenly appeared from nowhere. At any rate we did not discover it till it was right above the raft, either because of the brandy or because the pilot had intentionally hidden himself in the clouds as long as he could. The plane dived towards us in a graceful curve, and we returned the pilot's courtesy in the only way possible at the moment—that is, by raising our glasses and drinking to our unknown visitors. These seemed to want to keep us company, for the plane swept down towards us again and again like a weary sea-bird anxiously seeking a place to settle. Each time we caught a fleeting glimpse of several doubled-up figures with lifted cameras, so we concluded that it was a newspaper plane. Not till it had dived half a dozen times did it disappear.

Next day, March 26th, another aircraft appeared, and this time it was a seaplane of the Peruvian Navy that came to welcome us. And the following day a grey-painted patrol boat bore right down on us just as if her captain had had advance knowledge of our course and average speed, so we concluded that he was guided by a report from the pilot of the seaplane. Without asking our view of the matter, or offering any explanations, he made a sharp turn and sent a hawser over to us: after which he set his course for Callao, which was already just in sight behind the island of San Lorenzo. It seemed evident that Peruvian patrol boats were accustomed to towing rafts of prehistoric model. In spite of the Peruvians' undeniable skill we were glad that only ten miles separated us from the quay at Callao, for the towing was a trifle too fast for our taste, and the raft dipped her fore-deck under water again and again.

At the entrance to the harbour we were met by a motor boat with a full load of journalists and photographers, and a queer motor yacht with a double hull like a Polynesian canoe. The captain of the patrol boat told us that

Rapa Nui, as the queer motor yacht was called, was to take over the towing, and as we had no reason for objecting to this arrangement we obediently cast off the tow-rope. At the same moment the Press boat ran alongside the raft, and before we could utter a word of protest all the journalists and photographers had jumped on board. As we slowly approached the quay our uninvited guests began to pepper us with the most extraordinary questions. Eric, however, was in top form and had an answer for everything. Here are a few examples of his readiness.

'Why are you calling at Callao?'—'Because we didn't want to lose the pleasure of meeting you.'

'How much water have you left?'—'None. It came to an end the day before yesterday. But so long as a Frenchman has wine he needs no water.'

'Is anyone waiting for you here in Callao?'—'Yes, all the pretty women in Peru, I hope.'

'Why is the raft so low in the water?'—'Because you are weighing her down. She's meant for five persons, not fifty.'

We moored the raft at the Yacht Club's pier at 7 P.M. Our successful trial trip had thus taken forty-one days, which tallied exactly with Eric's estimate of from six to seven weeks made before we left Constitucion.

Next morning, to our undisguised astonishment, several of the papers of the Peruvian capital announced under large headlines that *Tahiti Nui II* had arrived at Callao in a sinking condition. One of the imaginative writers even went so far as to say that the raft would have sunk altogether if the voyage had lasted a few days longer.

When we saw the pictures which illustrated the articles we understood at once the cause of this absurd mistake. The journalists had seen the water washing over the deck while we were being towed, and had at once concluded that the raft had lain as low in the water before the towing began. After the towing ended they themselves had weighed the raft down so heavily that they got wet feet, and of course this had strengthened them in their mistaken idea. In reality the raft lay only about a foot deeper than when she left Constitucion, which was not disastrous in any way.

For safety's sake we inspected the raft thoroughly from stem to stern, and among other things we sawed in half one of the fifty cypress trunks which formed the body of the vessel. But nowhere did we find the slightest trace of ship-worms, which we feared most, and the trunk showed clearly that the sea water had penetrated the wood to the depth of only an inch or two, so that nine-tenths of it was still dry and hard. There was no doubt that the raft was still in first-class condition. But as, nevertheless, she lay a good deal deeper than we had orginally intended, and the waves had shown an unpleasant tendency to break into the cabin in a strong head wind, we decided to try to increase her buoyancy a little. Bamboos could not be obtained within a reasonable time, and we also sought balsa trunks in vain until the president of the Yacht Club hit upon the idea of advertising in the newspapers. Then a number of well-disposed people came to us with trunks which varied enormously in size, age and quality. We chose the twelve largest trunks, which even so were only about twelve feet long and about eight inches thick, and made them fast astern in the empty space between the cypress trunks and the deck. There was room for at least as many again, but unfortunately no more could be obtained.

At this juncture a Belgian chemist who lived in Lima, and had followed our proceedings with great interest from the start, said that we should supplement our rusty galvanized iron water drums with aluminium tanks. As he shrewdly pointed out, such tanks would be doubly useful to us on account of their durability, for as they became empty we could fasten them under the raft to increase her buoyancy. At first we thought this an unnecessary precaution, but when the Belgian kindly offered to get the tanks for us and the price proved to be one we could afford, we took his advice—primarily because our old drums were really in a wretched state. We thus became the possessors of no fewer than four forty-gallon and ten ten-gallon aluminium tanks, which actually was a good deal more than we needed. But Jean, who had just received two new heavy cases of oceanographical equipment, declared with a satisfied air that the surplus tanks would come in very handy for keeping fish, plankton and other kinds of marine life, so we filled only half the tanks with drinking water and wedged in the others, empty, under the after-deck on both side of the balsa trunks.

Most of our visitors, who were almost as numerous as at Constitucion, predicted many fearful disasters. But we had heard so many gloomy prognostications already that we paid no attention of them. The only brilliant exception was a cheerful curly-haired Czech, Eduardo Ingris, who from the very first was so enthusiastic that he even wanted to accompany us. Although we firmly refused to grant his wish, his confidence pleased us very much, for Ingris was the only one of all our visitors who had any previous experience of raft voyages. He had already in 1955 attempted to sail to the South Sea islands on a balsa raft of the *Kon-Tiki* type with the pretty name *Cantuta*, along with an Argentinian, a Dutchman, a Peruvian and an Indian girl from the vicinity of Lake Titicaca. But for some inexplicable reason this rather miscellaneous party started too late in the year from a place which lay too far north on the Peruvian coast, with the unfortunate result that the raft encountered adverse ocean currents which turned her into a merry-go-round for three months. The four men and the solitary woman were then picked up, emaciated and wearied, by an American warship.

Despite the unfortunate result of this ill-planned attempt Ingris was so eager to begin again that he came back every day and tried by new and ingenious arguments to persuade us to take him with us. Eric did for a short time seriously consider taking Ingris in place of Jean, but finally allowed such important considerations as Jean's general ability and usefulness to outweigh his personal antipathy to him and fortunately did not replace him.

As soon as we had examined the raft and increased her buoyancy to the best of our ability, we completed our preparations in great haste by purchasing with what little money we had left two cases of tinned beef, 180 lb. of potatoes, a generator ('used but in good condition') and ten gallons of petrol for it. Our haste was due not only to our intense longing for the peace and quiet of the sea after all the noise and bustle of Callao, but also, and in an even higher degree, to the fact that we had no time to lose if we wanted to reach the South Sea islands before the hurricane season began in October.

A Peruvian wireless fan presented us at the last moment with a new vertical aerial and kindly helped us to fit it to the mast. Not till the day before we sailed were we at last ready to test our wireless transmitters. We could only just hear our friend the wireless fan, who lived in one of the suburbs of Lima hardly five miles from the harbour, but both he and all other experts assured us emphatically that reception was always extraordinarily bad in a wide circle round Callao on account of certain magnetic disturbances, and that we should be able to talk to all the Peruvian stations without the least difficulty as soon as we escaped from the dead zone. To be on the safe side I made another attempt a couple of hours later and the result was rather better, which removed our last anxieties.

A whole fortnight earlier in the year—but eleven years later—than the *Kon-Tiki* expedition, we were towed out of Callao harbour about 11 A.M. on Sunday, April 13, 1958, and a few hours later were left to our fate in the strong Humboldt Current, which immediately took over the towing. Ingris endeavoured up to the last moment to persuade us to take him on as an extra hand.[1]

To avoid being swept far up towards Panama by the Humboldt Current, as *Cantuta* had been, we steered due west during the first days, which, as the deviation was strong, actually resulted in a very satisfactory west-north-westerly course. At the same time, being quite aware that ocean currents can be very capricious, we kept a sharp look-out for the dreaded Hormigas, two bare rocky islands lying in the middle of the Humboldt Current about fifty miles from Callao. When we passed them two days after we had sailed we were, not at all to our surprise, a good deal nearer to them than we had intended, and Eric expressed the feelings of the whole crew when he burst out in tones of relief:

'It's nice to know that whatever happens after this, there's no danger of our running ashore again during the next three months.'

'Another good thing is that we haven't any propeller to lose,' I added cheerfully.

I had suddenly remembered my eventful voyage in *Kaumoana* five years before.

We had arranged with a couple of Peruvian wireless fans to contact them every Thursday and Sunday. The first wireless day at sea was, therefore, Thursday, April 17th. I carefully primed the motor in plenty of time,

[1] Almost a year later to the day Ingris with one of his former and two new companions left Callao aboard a new balsa raft named *Cantuta II*, built after the same principles as *Kon-Tiki*. After an uneventful voyage the raft crash-landed three months later on a reef in the Tuamotu Group.

but however much I pulled the starting-rope at the appointed hour, it refused to start. I therefore took the whole motor to pieces well before the next contact was due, carefully examined all the parts and put it together again. The only reward for all these efforts was a few quickly suppressed coughing noises. We agreed at once with unanimity that we were still too near Callao to hear well, and we put away the generator and transmitter without regret.

About the same time—i.e., about a week after we had sailed—we changed—as easily and smoothly as a train changing tracks—from the Humboldt Current to the South Equatorial Current. All of a sudden the sea, hitherto a pale grey-green, became a bright dark blue, and began once more to swarm with tropical fish. We felt almost as if we were home already, for the waters round Tahiti are of this same colour. We cheerfully prepared our fishing gear. As usual, the dolphins were more numerous than all the other kinds put together, and on the first fishing day Jean spitted in a bare half-hour enough to have provided several solid meals for a crew ten times as large as ours. By degrees, however, he quite understandably grew tired of this rather dull sport, and let himself down into the sea with his spear-gun only when Juanito expressly asked for a fish. It was usually sufficient for Juanito to give his order five or ten minutes before dinner, just as he began to heat the frying-pan.

We had even less trouble when we wanted to feast on flying fish, for they came sailing on board of their own accord on their transparent, shimmering wing-fins. This happened especially at night, when our ship's light attracted them like a magnet, and we had only to turn them over and make our choice. Late one evening a long thin fish with sharp teeth followed the example of the flying fish and jumped on board. It proved on close examination to be a gempylus or snake mackerel—the strange deep sea fish of which only two specimens were known before the *Kon-Tiki* expedition. Jean was quick to stuff it into a container of formalin and assured us that he knew an ichthyologist who would be crazy with joy at this unique gift.

Jean's ichthyoligical friend would certainly have been at least as crazy—but not with joy—if he had seen what we did with another gempylus not long afterwards. When we found that these fish were continuing to jump on board we could at last no longer withstand the temptation to fry one. It tasted quite excellent, not unlike mackerel, and fried gempylus would certainly have been a standing dish on our menu if the supply had not suddenly run out. To make up for this we had more and more frequent visits from turtles, sharks and whales. Shark-catching was ridiculously easy, and we took many both on a hook and in a noose, but despite strenuous efforts on our part all the turtles which we tried to harpoon or catch with our hands in the Polynesian style escaped us at the last moment.

Not only did the ocean fauna round the raft resemble that which the *Kon-Tiki* men observed on their voyage, but life on board also followed the same pattern to a surprising extent. As the weather was brilliantly fine without interruption, and at this time the raft was still steering herself, we had so much time off that our voyage could without any exaggeration be called a holiday cruise. The only one of us who really had exacting and regular work to do was Jean, who daily made observations, took samples of water and collected plankton with incredible energy. Hans sometimes helped him, but killed most of the time in his own special way by random reading of the numerous philosophical and mathematical books which he had brought with him.

I myself discussed navigation and anthropology with Eric all round the clock, and, when he saw that his circle of listeners had widened, he could sometimes be induced to tell some splendid stories of his eventful life. Juanito had only one occupation when off duty: he slept as if he had been attacked by sleeping sickness during our stay in Callao. Now and again we turned on our wireless receiver to divert ourselves with a little music, but as a rule we were obliged to turn it off again quickly because our tastes were so different that music which delighted some was found unbearable by the rest.

Once in the middle of May we happened to pick up an American news bulletin, which to our surprise was mostly about France. According to the announcer Algeria was in a state of complete rebellion and, what was worse, the rebellion threatened to spread to the rest of France at any moment. It is significant of our mental state at this time that we took this disturbing news very calmly. Shame to say, I think my first feeling was one of thankfulness at being in safety on a raft on the other side of the globe, and it seemed that my two countrymen Eric and Jean shared this feeling. As for Juanito and Hans, they were of course, like all true South Americans, incapable of taking either their own or other people's revolutions seriously.

In Han's well-stocked library there was a copy—in German—of Thor Heyerdahl's book on the *Kon-Tiki* expedition, and of course we were not slow to make a number of comparisons. As everyone knows, the *Kon-Tiki* men wanted to prove that it was possible to sail from South America to Polynesia on a balsa raft, but it really made no difference to them at which of the many Polynesian islands they ended their voyage. We, on the other hand, were firmly resolved to reach Tahiti, and therefore kept a rather more northerly course than our predecessors to avoid the insidious coral reefs of the Tuamotu group. But this did not prevent us from comparing their daily runs with our own. We soon found to our satisfaction that we were keeping up at least as good a speed as the *Kon-Tiki* raft, i.e., thirty-five to fifty miles a day, and from May 11th, when I rigged up an extra square sail made of two foresails sewn together, our daily runs were regularly a little longer than our rival's. The member of our crew who took most interest in this original race with eleven years' difference in time was, quite understandably, the engineer Hans, and I grew by degrees firmly convinced that he had brought the *Kon-Tiki* book with him solely for the sake of the mathematical diversion which he had foreseen he could obtain with its help. Every time I took the altitude of the sun Hans appeared, slide-rule in hand, and carefully worked out, first, our average speed since we left Callao and then the probable date of our arrival at Tahiti if we continued to maintain exactly the same speed—which of course we never did. How seriously Hans took this mathematical game was shown clearly by his losing his appetite and becoming really unpleasant to deal with after I had—to the ill-concealed delight of all the others—pulled his leg by giving him wrong positions for a whole week.

The only clouds which darkened our existence during this part of the voyage were a bit of trouble with the steering and continued difficulty in starting the generator. The main reason for the raft not keeping a course as well as we had expected was that we were altogether too few to be able to manage the fourteen large heavy centre-boards—six forward and eight aft—as quickly and skilfully as the situation sometimes required. When I built the raft at Constitucion, warned by my experience on the outward voyage with *Tahiti Nui I,* I had placed a rudder astern as a necessary precaution. All the way up to Callao, and during the first part of our voyage in *Kon-Tiki*'s wake, we had left the fixed rudder alone and it had simply served as an extra centreboard. But now that, near the ninetieth degree of longitude, the raft was no longer keeping as good a course on account of the heavier sea, we simply loosened the rudder, nailed a tiller to the upper part of it and began to take turns at the helm. But these gave us little trouble, and to tell the truth we regarded them almost as pleasant breaks in our rather monotonous holiday life.

As for the big wireless transmitter, we waited till May 15th before making a fresh attempt to contact our Peruvian friends, who by then must have become very impatient. Our stubborn toil with the generator at last bore fruit, for it started at once with a dull mutter and continued to work perfectly. But this did not help us much, for now, for a change, there was trouble not only with the big transmitter, but also with the little one.

'Haven't I been saying all the time that we've been throwing away a heap of money quite unnecessarily on new-fangled follies?' said Eric ironically. 'I've never had any wireless of any sort on my earlier voyages, and I've got on just as well without it. Don't let us bother any more about the wretched transmitters, and let us console ourselves with the thought that we should never have any more peace if we did manage to get them going!'

We others objected that wireless apparatus were sometimes not quite useless at sea: for example, we should have gone to the bottom with our first bamboo raft if we had not had a transmitter on board. Eric was compelled to admit that. But, as he quite rightly pointed out at once, there was no danger of our meeting with gales like that in the sunny latitudes where we now were. Could we not see with our own eyes that the wind and currents were pushing us along in the right direction, and grasp the simple truth that it would not be very long before we arrived? So why were we worrying so much about such a trivial thing? For that matter, Eric added with his usual completely groundless optimism, we might soon meet a ship which would undertake to tell our friends that all was well on board.

As the spoilt child of fortune that he was, he was right, and to his great satisfaction it was he himself who, on the afternoon of May 26th, first sighted a cargo ship overhauling us. At first we were convinced that he was trying to pull our legs, but when at last we loafed out through the cabin door we could doubt no longer, for the steamer was right on top of us. We saluted according to the current regulations for sea travel by dipping our ensign twice, and the steamer not only answered, but altered her course and steered towards us. We now saw that she was *Pioneer Star*, an American ship which calls at Papeete at long intervals. The captain slowed down a cable's length away and hailed us through his megaphone. We waved cheerfully to him and to all the crew and passengers who were hanging over the rail, and Eric shouted as loud as he could:

'Please tell our friends in Papeete that all are well on board *Tahiti Nui II*.'

The captain seemed to have understood our messages despite the noise of the engines and the splashing of the waves, for he raised his hand, put on speed and continued his routine voyage towards our common destination beyond the horizon to westward.

Our meeting with *Pioneer Star* took place in 110°36′ west by 3°25′ south, i.e., exactly halfway between Callao and Papeete, so we had covered the first half of our voyage in six weeks. In view of the evenness and strength of the trade winds in eastern Polynesia it was not unreasonable to hope, as we all did, that we should be able to complete the second half of the voyage at least as quickly. This meant that we should arrive just in time for the French national day, which in Tahiti is always celebrated with the longest and merriest festivities of the year.

Chapter 5

WET FEET

The day after our meeting with *Pioneer Star* it rained for the first time since we left Callao. It was a fine drizzle, and did not last long enough for us to replenish our water supplies, which were getting low. But we were glad of it all the same, for we regarded it as a friendly reminder from the gods of the weather that they had not forgotten us and would soon send us more and heavier showers. Immediately afterwards we got a strong favourable wind, and for several days on end it continued to blow so steadily and well that we were doing between two and two and a half knots. Consequently our spirits were very high when we drank our usual Saturday *apéritif* on the after-deck on May 31st, and our lively conversation was almost entirely about our festal arrival at Tahiti.

During the night the wind increased further in

strength, which at first only pleased us. But when daylight came and we saw that the bow had been forced down a good four inches below the surface by the violent pressure of the wind on the sails, we immediately became rather worried and hastened to move the heaviest tanks and cases from the fore- to the after-deck. This improved matters a good deal, but the fore-deck was still not really clear of water. We were sure that the raft would straighten herself and resume her normal horizontal position if we struck or reefed the sails, but we all preferred wetting our feet a little to reducing our good speed, the more so when the midday observation on June 2nd showed that we had covered as much as eighty miles during the last twenty-four hours, which was several miles better than our previous record.

As we should have anticipated, even in our excited state, our violent driving of the raft came to a quick end, which could easily have taken a tragic turn. During a squall in the night of June 4th–5th, while Juanito was on watch alone, the raft suddenly swung broadside to the sea and immediately took a heavy list.

'Take in all sail, double quick,' Eric ordered. He had grasped the situation as soon as he awoke.

We dashed out on deck with the water splashing round our legs and tried to grasp the slippery sheets and flapping sails. I had just managed, after a violent struggle, to untie a knot on my side of the cabin when I heard a thud from the other side. At the same moment someone yelled:

'Man overboard!'

I splashed across the deck as quickly as I could and

almost knocked Jean over; he was vainly searching for a rope to use as a life-line. It was of course that unpractical, clumsy Hans who had been struck by the mainsail and had tumbled in. It was blowing half a gale, and the sea was roaring and hissing. Han's situation seemed hopeless, especially as the sky was covered with black clouds and visibility was bad. I searched the storm-lashed sea despairingly with my eyes, while Jean, swearing fiercely, disentangled the long rope which he had found at last.

A whimpering sound near my feet made me lower my eyes. It was Hans clinging with all his might to one of the trunks in the raft's side. Evidently he had had sufficient presence of mind to grasp the first object his hands had touched after his fall. Next moment a big wave came rolling along and bumped violently against the raft. More by luck than by skill Jean and I managed to haul Hans on board at the moment when, half conscious and exhausted, he was losing his grip. When he came to himself in the cabin he complained of a severe pain in one leg, but fortunately it did not seem to be broken. We gave him a good drink from our last bottle of whisky and had a long swig ourselves to help us forget this unpleasant incident.

Richly endowed now with all the wisdom and caution which only experience, it seems, can give, we stowed away the mainsail and set the much smaller spanker in its place. Immediately afterwards we set the foresail, too, so that the raft might keep her course more easily. We were glad to see that our speed was only slightly reduced, for we continued to make daily runs of from fifty to sixty miles.

A few days later—to be exact, on June 7th—immediately after darkness had fallen, we again had to take in all sail in a hurry, but this time for a quite different reason. Juanito had just taken over the helm, and the rest of us had turned in. Just as I was shutting my eyes and falling asleep I heard him shout:

'A light, a light quite near, to port!'

We could tell at once from his trembling, excited voice that it could not be a joke, so we dashed outside just as we were, dressed, half-dressed, or quite undressed. The light was white and strong and, as Juanito had said, quite close, not more than 300 yards ahead of us at an angle on the windward side. To reduce the deviation we struck the few sails we had up, after which I took out my electric torch and began to signal our raft's name and destination. Although I received no answer, I continued to flash signals with my torch as we slowly approached the mysterious light. We now saw that it was quite near the surface of the sea, so it could hardly be a ship's light: besides, a ship would certainly have been better lighted. Perhaps it was a sailing boat? We shouted and yelled as loud as we could, but received no answer. As I have already explained, we could not tack against the wind, and therefore, to our annoyance, we finally passed on the lee side of the still brightly shining light at a distance of only thirty yards, without being able to solve the mystery. We reluctantly set sail again and proceeded westward.

During the eager discussion which naturally followed Hans maintained that the light had come from a drifting ship's boat with some poor shipwrecked devils on board, so exhausted that they could not answer our signals, if they had not already died of hunger and thirst. I for my part inclined more to Eric's considerably less romantic theory that it was a Japanese fishing buoy, and this theory received further confirmation when, soon afterwards, we sighted first two similar lights and then, at a great distance, an illuminated boat of the kind which the Japanese use for tunny-fishing. I knew very well that the Japanese fish intensively in international waters in the western part of the Pacific. But that they now came all the way from Japan to lay their nets in the eastern part of the Pacific, 2000 miles from the nearest land, was definitely news to me, and testified to infinitely greater daring and enterprise than I thought them capable of. When would the United States, Colombia, Ecuador, Peru and France, all of whom had many ports in that part of the Pacific, at last dare to follow the Japanese example? I felt a new urge to realize an old dream and smiled with pleasure at the picture of myself as the well-to-do skipper of a fishing boat with a Tahitian crew and Tahiti as home port.

Before we had really got over the events of the night we had a new and considerably more disagreeable surprise: the rudder-post broke in two during the morning watch. It was simpler to make a new rudder than to mend the old one (which was, moreover, too small) so we pulled up three of the six centreboards in the bows and nailed them together. It took us a day and a half to make and fix the giant new rudder, which when complete weighed about 125 lb. and was at least twice as large as the old one, but when the laborious job was finished we found to our satisfaction that the raft answered the helm a good deal better than before. Despite this, much more muscle power than before was of course required to handle it. To economize our strength as much as possible we installed an ingenious steering system of tackles and ropes, which worked very well. To perfect this we also turned a few more centreboards into a platform for the unfortunate helmsman to stand on, so that he should no longer be in danger of being washed away when the waves broke over the stern, which had happened rather often of late.

We were still in a beggarly 4° south, and if we were to reach Tahiti, which lay in 17° south, we must without delay swing down in a wide curve to the south-west. The raft should really have followed this course almost of her own accord, for according to all charts and navigational handbooks the South Equatorial Current ought to turn off to the south immediately after 120° west longitude, and at the same time the trade winds should follow from this degree of longitude a similar circular course. But for some mysterious reason we still met with only northerly currents long after we had passed 120° west, and the wind too behaved abnormally by ceaselessly changing its direction. Laying the helm over to starboard did not help much, but by quickly taking in sail every time the wind was south-easterly and setting sail again just as quickly as soon as the wind went round into the north-east, we actually succeeded in gradually making a few degrees to southward. But this was a fearfully tiring method, and as all hands had to turn out frequently all round the clock, we got no proper sleep. All the time the raft continued to sink, slowly, but inexorably.

The only real distraction during this trying time was a short visit from a whale shark as big as the raft. (Whale sharks are the world's largest fish and have been aptly so called because they are often as big as whales.) The brown monster swam level with the raft without the slightest exertion, and nosed at it long and inquisitively with its horrid snout before hurrying on westward at top speed with a contemptuous flick of its tail. I could not restrain a slightly ironical smile. Evidently we were copying the *Kon-Tiki* expedition in everything—except the raft's ability to float.

In the middle of June we had nearly eight inches of water in the cabin. We therefore raised the lower bunks by this amount, but the water splashed about so violently and made everything so damp that we all, whether we had upper or lower bunks, preferred to establish ourselves on the only dry place that remained—the cabin roof. For once in a way my shipmates had a few words of praise for the creator of the raft, and I was equally pleased that, by a lucky inspiration, I had had a flat roof made instead of a pointed one as on *Tahiti Nui I*. The roof was not more than 10 feet by 13 feet, but we actually suffered much less from crowding than from the wind, which, strange as it may seem, was often unpleasantly chilly at night. This change was particularly unwelcome to Eric, whose strength had begun to fail even before we moved up on to the roof. As during the outward voyage from Tahiti to Chile, he seemed to be simply tired and exhausted, for he had no pain anywhere, and although we examined him and questioned him thoroughly we could not find a single clear symptom of any definite sickness. We knew from experience that his condition could easily be made worse if he got cold and wet, so we made a little tent for him out of a piece of canvas and tried for his sake to be glad that the keenly desired, thirst-quenching rain seemed not to be coming at all.

As early as June 20th we saw clearly that we no longer had any prospect of reaching Tahiti unless we got a strong northerly wind for two or three weeks on end, and of course it was useless to hope for such a fantastic piece of luck. But we were only 400 miles from the Marquesas Islands, were well placed for reaching them, and were still doing about fifty miles a day with only spanker and foresail set. So we were still in good heart. But only a few days later there came a disastrous change for the worse, when the wind, hitherto so variable, began to blow steadily from the wrong quarter, the south-east, and gradually increased in strength. We took in all sail, hoisted a little storm foresail in the bows and laid the heavy rudder over. Despite this it was not long before the rough pencil line which marked our route began to point due west—past the Marquesas Islands.

One day after another dragged on without appreciable change in the course of our long drift. But it was not till the night of June 26th–27th, when I was standing on watch alone on the slippery platform aft, that I began to be really downhearted. Again and again I looked anxiously at the compass to see if it was really true that the wind was still south-easterly. Every time I was obliged sadly to admit that it was. Should we miss the Marquesas too? I dared not think what the consequences might be.

Suddenly I gave a start. I had clearly felt the raft sinking under my feet, swiftly and cruelly. Next moment a wave washed over the platform on which I stood. I clung fast to the cabin and waited for the water to drain away. But strange to say it did not do so. Then the truth dawned on me. The raft had not been simply forced down under water by a violent squall, but had suddenly for some reason lost a large part of her buoyancy. As the water now covered the platform, the raft must have sunk nearly three feet. This dismal sight brought back to mind the advice which one of the owners of the yard at Constitucion had given me while the raft was being built, when he had seen me covering the deck with plaited work of Chilean willow.

'Don't forget to water the deck regularly,' he had said. 'Plaited work like that splits if it is too dry.'

My first thought was to call out all hands at once. But a second later it occurred to me that it was kinder to let them sleep on. They would probably take the disaster better in daylight than if I woke them in the middle of the night. And indeed, they all showed extraordinary self-control when they let themselves down from the roof one after another in the pallid dawn. We discussed at length what could be the reason for the rapid fall in the raft's buoyancy, and we finally decided on a close examination of the cypress trunks. After great exertions I succeeded, with Jean's help, in cutting one of the trunks in the bows. We saw at first glance that the stump we had cut off was bored through and through by ship-worms. When we threw it into the sea it sank like a stone. All the trunks we examined were quite as worm-eaten. When we waded into the cabin, which was now more like a swimming pool than anything else, we found to our disgust that a great deal of our provisions and gear had been washed away. We therefore hastened to lift up all the remaining cases, parcels and apparatus into the upper berths or make them fast to the roof.

It was serious enough that the raft had sunk almost three feet, but what was much worse for the moment was that she was again becoming extremely difficult to steer. One or two of my shipmates therefore began to wonder if there was really any object in continuing the tiring watches at the helm. To my great surprise Eric agreed with them, and his argument was typical of his whole philosophy.

'My experience is that it is a pure waste of one's strength to try to fight against the forces of Nature,' he said, smiling gently, 'for they are always stronger than we are. What did the old Polynesian seadogs do when they ran into a storm? They simply lay down to sleep, full of confidence that their sea god Taaroa would help them. So let us, in Polynesian fashion, spare our strength for the days to come when we may need it more, and let the raft drift where she likes. Perhaps Taaroa will help us too. . . .'

I admitted that Eric's proposal was much more sensible than it sounded; yet, having thoroughly weighed the pros and cons, I decided to vote against it. I feared that waiting passively for an uncertain outcome would make us so listless and dull-witted that we should end by becoming quite indifferent to our fate. The Polynesian way was no doubt excellent for Polynesians, but we Westerners had not the same fatalistic outlook, and as in the navy discipline and routine were certainly the best way of keeping up our morale. I did my best to carry conviction and strenuously urged that we should continue to steer as southerly a course as possible, as all hope of reaching the Marquesas Islands had not yet disappeared. I concluded as follows:

'Even if we miss the Marquesas, we have still a good chance of reaching one of the northernmost atolls in the Tuamotu group or one of the most westerly of the Society Islands. On the other hand, if we let the raft drift before the winds and currents, it is absolutely certain already that we shall just go on through empty sea.'

'I understand you very well, and it shall be as you wish,' Eric said in a spiritless voice when I had finished. 'I am old, tired and ill, and it is not right of me to try to force my will. I therefore hand over the command to you, Alain, so from now on you will take all important decisions. It is a great and heavy responsibility, and that is why I have waited so long before turning it over to you. But I think it would be still more irresponsible conduct to try to go on playing a part for which I have no longer the strength.'

Frankly speaking, I would rather have been appointed captain under rather more favourable conditions and preferably on a more seaworthy craft. But as I was the only one who could navigate a vessel, I had as little choice as Eric. I therefore bowed to his will and concluded the discussion by urging yet again that we should continue the steering watches.

No further objection was offered, but Juanito soon showed his dissatisfaction in a particularly unpleasant manner. Again and again when he was on watch he let the raft swing broadside on to the sea. Each time she did this she took such a list that we nearly fell into the water, and to crown everything we were generally obliged to fiddle with the rudder and fight with the flapping sails for hours on end to force the raft back on to her proper course. When we abused Juanito he only answered carelessly that it was not his fault and that he did his best. Of course this only made us angrier, with the unexpected result that Juanito suddenly refused to be cook any longer. When he persisted in his decision despite all our efforts to make him see reason, Jean good-naturedly offered to take over the thankless post of cook. (So as not to make the raft more unsteady, we had not moved our heavy gas cooker on to the roof but left it in the cabin, where it was now wetter than ever.) But becoming cook did not prevent Jean from fishing, and he jumped into the sea with an energy that made us marvel as soon as he had a little time to spare. But unfortunately the result of all his exertions was nil. For some reason or another all the dolphins and other eatable fish had disappeared. On the other hand, a large brown shark was following us faithfully, day after day.

To my boundless joy it looked for a short time as if I was going to be right, for during the first three or four days after the vital council we again approached the Marquesas Islands, kindly helped, I suppose, by a south-going ocean current. But as early as June 29th it was clear to us all that we should miss them in spite of this welcome aid. Nor in all probability should we reach any islands in the Tuamotu or Society groups, if the wind did not soon become more favourable. The next group of islands in the direction in which we were drifting consisted of the three widely separated atolls Caroline, Vostok and Flint, and they were about 600 miles away. If we missed them too we should have to go on for at least another 1200 miles to Samoa, or . . . No, farther than that we dared not think. In any case it was safest to prepare for a long voyage. But how?

'Increase the raft's buoyancy, make her steadier, and ration food and water,' came in a faint voice from Eric's berth.

The solution which Eric advocated was roughly the same as what the rest of us already had in mind, so for once we were all in agreement. After a short discussion we agreed that the best way to make the raft lighter and steadier was to cut away one of the mizzen-masts (I use the plural because we had a double mast which looked like an inverted V), the sails of which we had long before transferred to the mainmasts. When we had carried this out with good results, we set about making an inventory of food stores. We still had plenty of rice, flour and macaroni. As far as we could estimate, it looked as if our stock of these would last for at least another two months. We had also thirty tins of condensed milk, thirty packets of raisins, seven pots of honey, twelve tins of preserved meat and as many of fruit, a good many pounds of lentils and sugar, a little chocolate powder and a very little tea. As for coffee, a kind manufacturer of the powdered variety had presented us with as many as 500 tins, and we still had so many left that we simply had not the energy to count them.

But although we could make our foodstuffs last a considerable time by rationing ourselves at once, our supply of drinking water gave us serious worry. Of the 100 gallons of drinking water which we had taken on board before we left Callao only fifteen gallons remained; for, contrary to our expectations, no proper rain had fallen during the two and a half months which had passed since then. If we went on consuming a gallon a day, as we had done hitherto, our water would not last for more than a week. The situation was especially critical because Eric now had a temperature in addition to his other troubles and was always thirsty. We reluctantly reduced the daily water ration to just over a pint for Eric and two-thirds of a pint for the rest of us, and began to mix our rations with salt water. At the same time Jean hunted in his numerous cases to see if he had enough tubes and scraps of metal to make a distilling apparatus. He quickly found heaps of test tubes and queer gadgets, and tackled his difficult task with determination.

On July 1st we passed Eiao, the northernmost island in the Marquesas group, at a distance of only thirty-five miles. A crowd of white seabirds, which evidently nested on the uninhabited rocky island, cruised round the raft for several hours, but returned to their home with mocking farewell cries when the dusk fell. We would have given much to have been able to follow their example, but the raft was as usual a helpless victim of the winds and currents and drifted slowly westward.

To disperse my gloomy thoughts I dipped a little that evening into the splendid book about Eric's first long voyage in the Pacific with Tati which François de Pierrefeu produced in 1938. Suddenly my eyes fell upon the following passage:

'Eric's leading star shines over the Marquesas Islands. He has known intuitively from his earliest youth that his real Oceanic home is there, and that the thread of his destiny will some day lead him there as the fates have decreed. While waiting for this remote day to dawn he will spend the time with strings of adventures and mad pranks at innumerable other places on the earth's surface, far from the place where the 10th degree of latitude cuts the 140th degree of longitude: it is there, however, that his final destiny will be decided.'

How had anyone been able to make so correct a prophesy twenty years before, and what was the destiny that awaited Eric—and perhaps the rest of us on board the sinking raft? I read the prophetic words over and over again in silence, and every time I felt more and more uneasy. I shut the book and hurried out on deck to keep an eye on Juanito so that he should not let the raft turn round again unnecessarily.

On July 2nd the wind moderated slowly, and as we slid slowly on over long gentle rollers the burning sun rose again into the sky, which was quite cloudless for the first time in several weeks. Our water ration of two-thirds of a pint represented no more than two cups a day, and although we mixed it with larger and larger quantities of sea water and drank it in gulps, it came nowhere near quenching our thirst. To lose as little bodily moisture as possible, at my suggestion, we put on wet shirts and trousers, and took a dip in the sea as soon as the clothes began to dry. Jean was working hard at his distilling apparatus all the time, but as he had not the right tools he made little progress.

After two more burning days I called a ship's council. Jean, Hans, Juanito and I were still in comparatively good fettle and could certainly hold out as long as the water lasted, that is, for at least two or three more weeks. But Eric's condition was growing rapidly worse: indeed, he now had difficulty in swallowing without help of small quantities of honey and condensed milk which constituted his only food. It was very problematical how long the raft would remain afloat, and the distances between the few islands were very great. We therefore decided, mainly for Eric's sake, to make a fresh attempt with our wireless apparatus and send out SOS signals at once while we were still in waters where there were plenty of schooners and other vessels which could quickly come to our help.

According to the wireless handbook all stations all over the world listened in for SOS signals at every complete hour for ten minutes, so I set up both wireless transmitters on the roof and in good time for 7 P.M. started the motor which was fortunately still well primed. But, as had happened before, the dials of the large transmitter did not move. Convinced that it would be a waste of time and effort to continue transmitting with a completely dead apparatus, I exchanged it for Roland d'Assignies's specially-constructed little Morse transmitter which had saved our lives once before at the Juan Fernandez Islands. When I turned it on, I found the batteries still in good order. Full of expectancy I began to tap out our position —70° 20′ south latitude by 141° 15′ west longitude—followed by three dots, three dashes and three dots.

Although I had not heard as much as a click in my earphones to indicate that anyone had intercepted our distress signal, I was just as expectant when I repeated my SOS at 8 P.M. Jean and Hans, who sat near enough to the little paraffin lamp for their expressions to be visible, looked cheerful and hopeful. (Eric was asleep in his tent at the opposite corner of the roof and Juanito was at the helm.) But suddenly they looked terrified and clutched at each other. Next moment I myself had a horrible feeling in the pit of the stomach and fell over backwards. I had slipped halfway down the roof when I recovered and managed to cling to a cross-rib. The raft had now so heavy a list that I had the greatest difficulty in clambering up the sloping roof again and making fast the wireless apparatus and other loose objects. When I had done this I began to look round angrily for the helmsman, Juanito, since there was scarcely any doubt that it was his fault that we had almost capsized. I told him off with feeling and conviction and with the wholehearted support of the rest, but as on previous occasions when he had endangered our lives by his carelessness he said nothing, but merely shrugged his shoulders.

He was relieved at the helm as a precaution, after which Jean and I went on sending out SOS signals at hourly intervals until dawn, but without response.

We hastened to look into the cabin to see if all was in order. The sight that met our eyes was deplorable. Not only the food supplies and all our personal belongings, which we had thought were secure in the upper berths, but also a cine camera, a sextant and some of Jean's oceanographic apparatus, which we had tied firmly to the roof, had tumbled down and were chaotically rolling to and fro in three feet of water. Even more depressing was the discovery that one of our two small ten-gallon containers of drinking water was also floating about lidless and empty among the packets of biscuits and clothes. I gave Juanito another rocket, but the only result was that he suddenly refused to do any more watches at the helm.

With one sick man and one striker on board, and water for ten days at most, it was more than ever necessary that we should be relieved, and Jean and I, with the courage of despair, went on calling for help for two more days and nights, now with one and now with the other transmitter.

But finally we were forced to admit what from mistaken consideration for one another we had so long tried to conceal—that the wireless transmitters were not working.

What were we to do now?

Jean and Hans proposed that we should build a boat and sail, or even row, back to the Marquesas Islands. I immediately tried to counter this wild proposal with the, in my opinion, quite conclusive argument that we had neither tools nor material for boat-building and that, even if we succeeded in making something resembling a boat, we could not possibly sail or row back to the Marquesas, i.e., against the wind and the ocean currents. But these elementary truths did not greatly impress them, landlubbers as they were, so our futile debate continued. It was Eric who finally brought it to an end by quite unexpectedly repeating in a feeble voice his previous advice:

'Increase the raft's buoyancy again, make her steadier, and ration water and food still more strictly!'

We could hear clearly that he was impatient that we found it so hard to learn such a simple lesson. To avoid objections he added a few more instructions:

'Throw all unnecessary gear overboard. Then cut away the mainmasts and rig up a smaller mast with a storm foresail.'

I was deeply grateful to Eric for this diversion. I obeyed immediately and began to fling overboard a quantity of useless personal belongings. The others followed my example after a little hesitation. When a little later we cut away the mainmasts this, to our surprise and pleasure, lightened the raft so much that the fore-deck again became visible.

'Good,' said Eric. 'Now let the raft drift where she likes and turn in. You're quite worn out from being up all the last few nights.'

I let him have his way on this point too—though I was firmly resolved that it was to be only a temporary concession—and for the first time since leaving Constitucion five months earlier we all took a watch off and had a full night's sleep. It did us an immense amount of good, and when we awoke we were full of courage and confidence—and also fearfully hungry and thirsty.

We kept a keen watch for fish, but as usual saw only the suspiciously sociable shark, which for that matter seemed as hungry as ourselves. But we quickly forgot the absence of filleted fish from our menu when in the course of that afternoon Jean at last completed the distilling apparatus on which he had been working for a week. The cooker's gas cylinders were disturbingly light, but we had also a Swedish Primus cooker aboard and ample supplies of paraffin, so we thereupon decided to reserve this for Jean's queer apparatus. Although the Primus had been neglected ever since we sailed from Constitucion, it began to work at once. Soon the heavy drops of water began to fall into a tin one after another with a cheerful splashing noise. Contrary to what might have been expected of a cooker so roughly used, it went on hissing as regularly and soothingly hour after hour, while the tin slowly filled to the brim. The water was cloudy and tasted strongly of tin, but all the same we agreed pathetically that it was the most delightful liquid we had ever drunk.

So far so good. But even if we had only a vague idea of the Primus cooker's fuel consumption, it was clear that our supply of paraffin, which was about six gallons, would not last for ever. This was all the more depressing because it now looked as if the voyage itself *would* last for ever. For several days our course had been *west-north-west,* so that we were on our way towards a particularly desolate part of the Pacific, where the small and mostly uninhabited atolls were so few in number and so widely scattered that we might go on for thousands of miles without seeing a single one.

Our situation was indeed so uncertain that we were compelled to make a further cut in our food rations. I therefore made a complete inventory of our stores for the second time in a fortnight. I had made a detailed list at the previous stocktaking and had noted every day how much of the various articles we had used: consequently I knew exactly how much should remain, and saw at once that we were short of five tins of condensed milk. I was furious and it was only with the greatest effort that I succeeded in controlling myself. I did not let the others see from my face that there was anything wrong, but as soon as I contrived to be alone with Eric I told him of my unpleasant discovery.

'It would only make matters worse to try to find the guilty person,' Eric said, after thinking the problem over for a few minutes. 'No one would confess, and the only consequence would be disturbing, quarrelling and general mistrust. So let us content ourselves with seeing that nothing of the kind happens again. Lock up all the food in one of the large cases which have padlocks. Serve the rations yourself. And I'll give you another bit of good advice. Stop the distilling apparatus at night. A distilling apparatus which is working twenty-four hours a day ought to give more water than ours does. I've been keeping an eye on it for the last few days, and the result is always worse at night, when most of us are asleep, than in the daytime, which seems uncommonly suspicious.'

I took his advice with a heavy heart, and it was not difficult to see that my shipmates were hurt by my unconcealed suspicions. But I agreed with Eric that we had practically no choice but to let the innocent and the guilty suffer alike.

I then urged stubbornly that we should rig up a little emergency mast, set sail and do steering watches again, as I still thought it bad for us to have nothing at all to do. Moreover, by steering a definite course we could at least prevent the raft from turning round and laying herself broadside on to the sea. This in my opinion quite justified all the exertion involved, no matter where we ended up. Not only Jean and Hans, but also Juanito at last obeyed, though most reluctantly and without a spark of enthusiasm. Jean in particular, who till now had always been so smart, handy and helpful, seemed at a low ebb and just hung on to the tiller listlessly without making any real attempt to steer. But I myself was hardly brimming over with energy and *joie de vivre*.

On July 13th our morale touched bottom, from an apparently far-fetched but quite understandable cause. In

Tahiti every chance of amusement is always exploited to the uttermost and the Fourteenth of July festivities actually begin there the day before; we could not help thinking how differently we should have spent the day if our voyage had gone according to plan. After a long and obviously disapproving contemplation of our blank, gloomy faces, Eric beckoned to me late in the afternoon—he was too weak to be able to call out—and said curtly:

'Hoist an ensign at the masthead.'

I took it that he thought it would have a beneficial effect on our morale to see a Tricolor at the masthead, and although I was far from being optimistic, I dutifully carried out his wish.

It was just light the next morning when Hans, the steersman, woke us with a piercing cry:

'A ship, a ship!'

We stared sleepily in the direction in which Hans pointed. The incredible had happened. A large cargo ship was crossing our path at right angles, due astern, three miles away at most. I looked at Eric in surprise, and he smiled back mysteriously. Of course it could be nothing but pure chance that we had sighted a ship just after we had hoisted the ensign. But how was it that such strange coincidences occurred time after time during the two years I had spent with Eric—not to mention all the help which fortune had brought him in his life? If I had believed in any higher powers, I should certainly have long ago come to the conclusion that he was in league with them.

While these thoughts were flashing through my mind,

my comrades and I had taken off our Tahitian loin-cloths and begun to wave them. Immediately afterwards Jean, recovering his old energy and initiative, clambered up the mast like a squirrel and began to wave the flag. But no one on board the cargo ship seemed to notice us, although we were now so near that we saw she was one of the well-known New Zealand steamers which call regularly at Papeete on their shuttle service to Canada.

We quickly realized that waving loin-cloths was not enough if we wanted to be seen. Juanito and I suggested lighting a fire, and Jean and Hans were as ready as could be to help us carry out the plan. Luckily we had a large metal dish which Juanito had used for melting fat in the happy days when he was still our merry cheerful cook, and this we placed at once on the roof, after which we looked round for fuel. The only things we could find in a hurry were a few old ropes' ends. But they had to do. So we laid them on the bottom of the dish, soaked them in oil and set light to them. But to our great distress the wind immediately drove down the thick smoke which was developed. Eric, who seemed to have awakened from his previous drowsiness, had the idea of heliographing with a pocket mirror, and soon we were all signalling like mad with mirrors and pieces of glass.

All hands on board the cargo steamer had evidently, according to a good old nautical tradition, caroused so deeply during their stay at Tahiti that they were too tired and sleepy to notice a low-lying raft in the deeply indented sea landscape, and our saviours that might have been receded with tantalizing slowness till at last they disappeared beneath the horizon to the north-north-east.

When I slipped gloomily down from the roof to take the first morning watch I landed in water that reached high up my calves. There was no doubt that the raft was sinking rapidly.

Above: 'Tell our friends in Papeete that we are all well on board,' called Eric de Bisschop to the cargo ship *Pioneer Star,* which overtook *Tahiti Nui II* about halfway between South America and Polynesia on May 26, 1958. *Below:* When the raft really began to sink all hands moved up onto the roof, where Eric, who at that time was still in good form, hoisted his Royalist pennant half in fun and half in earnest.

Above: The raft sank gradually deeper and deeper, and it was impossible to prevent the waves from washing away the gear inside the cabin. *Below:* The raft soon became so unsteady that she repeatedly threatened to capsize. To keep her upright Jean (in the picture) and Alain helped one another to cut down the masts and make an outrigger in the Polynesian style.

Left: When at last *Tahiti Nui II* threatened to sink altogether, the unlucky crew built a smaller escape raft of wooden beams and empty tanks. *Below:* When Alain and his comrades had successfully placed Eric de Bisschop on board the escape raft, they spent several days swimming to and fro between the two rafts with provisions and equipment.

When free of her crew and most of the gear *Tahiti Nui II* became lighter for a short time, which made it easier to unship the outrigger and complete the emergency raft.

The very next day, when the desperate men were ready to cast off and try to reach land with their emergency raft, *Tahiti Nui II* had sunk so deep that she must have disappeared under the surface only a few hours later.

The last photograph of Eric de Bisschop. It can be clearly seen that he was worn out physically and tired to death.

Above: After a long search the crew found their emergency raft several miles from the scene of the disaster. Several of the tanks had broken loose and moreover the raft was bottom-up. *Below:* Among the few belongings which they found were their wireless receiver and the Polynesian wooden image which had been an ornament of *Tahiti Nui I* on the outward journey.

Above: The friendly inhabitants served up one huge banquet after another for the starving men, and a bevy of girls regularly undertook to brush away the flies for them. *Below:* In the village hall (note the Royal portraits on the wall) the secretary of the expedition, Carlos Garcia-Palacios, heartily thanked the inhabitants of Rakahanga for all their help.

Above: The natives, wearing their best Sunday clothes, carried Eric de Bisschop's body down to the shore, where a French patrol boat was waiting to take the surviving members of the expedition back to Tahiti. *Below:* Papeete at last! Alain, standing on the remains of the emergency raft in the French patrol boat's stern, again saw Tahiti, which he had left in such an exalted mood two years earlier on board *Tahiti Nui I*.

Bengt Danielsson met his friend Alain Brun on the quay.

Chapter 6

WE LOSE OUR BALANCE

As the raft sank deeper and deeper—which she did with alarming rapidity—she gradually became unsteadier and more difficult to steer. Although our desperate efforts to swing down to the south-west, where there were many inhabited islands, had no result whatever, and our actual course continued to be north-north-west, I would on no account give way to my shipmates' entreaties to let the raft drift. How right I was in insisting on this was shown as clearly as I could have desired during the night of July 16th–17th, when the rudder-post broke yet again. The raft had often heeled over before, so we were not at first unduly anxious when she immediately turned broadside on to the sea and took a heavy list. But when, instead of slowly righting herself, she continued her pendulum movement until we had the greatest difficulty in remaining on the roof, it became alarmingly clear to us that she had in only a few days lost a great deal more of her already very limited stability.

The only way of preventing the raft from capsizing altogether was, of course, to establish a counter-weight as quickly as possible. We soon found that it was not enough to crawl over to the windward side, so I began to move as much as possible of our gear and provisions across, while my shipmates hung as live weights along the cabin roof. It was fearfully exhausting on account of the steep slope of the deck, but I had the satisfaction of seeing the raft slowly recover her equilibrium.

We had now to resume our course without delay, and even this proved to be much more difficult than we had imagined. It was impossible to set the sail at an angle and make use of the wind, as we had so often done before with good results. We therefore made a long oar out of a slat and a plank so as to row stern up into the wind. But the oar was as heavy as lead, the aft platform was slippery and the raft unsteady, and only after several hours of hard toil were we at last able to shove the raft round so that her bows pointed westward again. After this we had to shift all the cargo again at top speed so that we should not heel over the other way. We spent the rest of the night repairing the rudder, while all the time the raft continuously threatened to turn round, for our only temporary means of steering were our heavy oar and our few remaining centreboards.

When the rudder was at last in place, towards noon the following day, the raft became fairly steady again, but it felt as if she had had a knock of some kind, for she lurched more violently than before and it was very difficult to steer a straight course. To avoid all further mishaps of this kind we agreed that in future we must keep a sharper look-out during our turns at the helm. Both Jean and Hans did their utmost, but strangely enough Juanito became increasingly careless and seemed, like the raft, to be in a fair way to losing his balance altogether.

The first warning that there was something seriously wrong with poor Juanito came shortly afterwards, when he quite unnecessarily let the raft turn round no less than three times during his turns at the helm. Each time we all but tumbled into the sea and had to toil like galley-slaves for hours to prevent a serious catastrophe. We were quite understandably in a towering rage and cursed him furiously. As under similar circumstances a few weeks earlier, Juanito was offended and refused point-blank to take any more watches. Jean, Hans and I were thoroughly sick of our problem child's stupidity. We decided, therefore, to act in future as if Juanito no longer existed and quietly divided the watches between ourselves.

Instead of resigning himself to this indulgent decision, Juanito quite unexpectedly began to hold forth, declaring that he wanted to build a boat and clear out. He took good care not to say where he would go, but he decribed eloquently and in detail the boat he meant to build (framework of eucalyptus wood and bottom and sides of masonite) and confidently asserted that it would be possible to do at least four knots with such a boat. To my infinite annoyance Jean and Hans—who had considered similar plans directly after we had missed the Marquesas Islands

—listened eagerly to this lunatic proposal and almost seemed to be taking it seriously. Eric and I had secretly discussed every conceivable plan for saving ourselves a long time before, just to know how to answer our over-optimistic shipmates on occasions like this, and we had come to the conclusion that only if we passed very close to an island, and of course on the windward side of it, would there be some sense in building a small escape craft, more like a raft than a boat, and venture on a sailing race with death. I now expounded this view in detail, emphasizing that apart from the difficulty of building a suitable craft it was still much too early to try to abandon the raft, as it was at least 300 miles to the nearest island, Caroline, and we seemed to be moving away from it.

I had hoped that my diplomatic speech, which showed that I was not all opposed to their plans in principle, but only wanted to wait for the right moment to try to carry them out, would fall on good soil. But I was speaking to ears that would not hear, and, much as I disliked worrying Eric, I had to ask him to let us know in plain language what he thought of Juanito's proposal. Unfortunately he was more ill and tired than usual, for he only replied in a feeble voice:

'Do what you like, but I'm staying here on board *Tahiti Nui II.*'

I declared emphatically that I meant to stay on board like Eric, which meant that if the three members of the boat-building party persisted in their plans they would have to do without a navigator. Jean and Hans then at last saw reason. Juanito, on the contrary, seemed absolutely furious at the turn events had taken, and after sulking for a long time in one corner of the roof he suddenly rose and grimly announced that he meant to throw our provisions and our water overboard, 'so that there may be an end to our sufferings for good and all.'

A few threatening gestures were enough to make him desist from this plan, but it was clear that we should have to keep a close watch on him in future. For that matter, his abnormally large, bloodshot eyes showed more clearly than all his words and action that there was something wrong with poor Juanito's mind. I spent a very uneasy and sleepless night, but when daylight returned Juanito, who strange to say had slept well all night, seemed much calmer. Eric with wonderful self-control had a long and comradely talk with him, after which he promised to behave properly, but curiously enough did not consider that this meant helping with the steering watches or resuming his duties as cook. As he clearly could no longer be relied on, and was rather a hindrance than a help to us in our work, we made no objections.

Soon, however, Juanito's conscience seemed to be troubling him, for I often noticed him slyly following our activities with guilty looks. Two days later he was no longer able to endure doing nothing, for he slipped down from the roof and asked politely if he could not help me to raise the floor in the cabin, a most necessary piece of work which I had just begun. Of course I nodded encouragingly, and he gave me excellent help.

But the very next day things were all wrong again. This time Juanito was discontented with the rationing.

He was particularly annoyed at not getting any honey. If he had complained that the food was monotonous and rations small I should not have been much surprised. If he had asked to have more water, because he was dying of thirst, I should have understood him still better, for the distilling apparatus had been broken several days before and all our attempts to repair it had failed. But to worry about honey, which only makes one more thirsty, was absolutely irrational.

The only conceivable explanation was that Juanito in this indirect manner was aiming at Eric, whose sole food still consisted of honey and condensed milk. I was therefore about to refuse his mean request with the contempt it deserved when, to my utter astonishment, Jean and Hans sided with Juanito and also demanded that we should share out the remaining seven pots of honey among ourselves. In this case too their action appeared to be primarily a more or less conscious protest against Eric for the expedition having taken such a disastrous turn.

I saw at once that it was useless to try to explain that strict rationing was in everyone's interest and that in the name of justice Eric was obviously entitled to all the honey and more condensed milk than the rest of us, seeing that he ate no other food at all. In the malignant frame of mind in which my comrades were, no explanations could possibly lead to anything but quarrelling and perhaps to even worse disputes, which might have catastrophic results, since in our perilous situation it was absolutely vital to stick together and help one another. So without saying a word I produced three pots of honey and gave one to each of them. But I soon began to regret my weakness, not so much for Eric's sake, for there were four pots left, but on grounds of discipline.

Only a few hours later I had clear proof of how dangerous it was to set foot on the comfortable path of concessions, and this time too Juanito was the chief actor in a still more unpleasant drama.

Although Juanito had just been urging that the rations were too small, he quite illogically refused to eat when Jean served up fresh tunny and biscuits for dinner. Of course this was a caprice which did us no harm, and we only shrugged our shoulders at it. After watching us gloomily as we ate he suddenly got up, took an axe out of the tool-box and slid down from the roof. Still without saying a word, he laid himself on his stomach in the water and cut off the eucalyptus bowsprit which, like the masts, we had made fast along the side of the raft.

As if by secret agreement, we all looked the other way, as if indifferent and uninterested, while in reality we were wondering what on earth we were to do. I quickly came to the conclusion that I must stop Juanito at once, in order to put an end once and for all to the dangerous delusion which unfortunately seemed to be gaining ground on board—namely, that everyone could do as he liked. But at the same time I saw that I might have a better chance of success if I did not set about it too brusquely and violently. So I said to Jean in a loud voice:

'If it isn't too much for you, Jean, I'd like you to make another oar. We need a reserve oar in case the one we're using should get broken.'

Jean understood what I meant at once. He slipped down from the roof and began to examine the eucalyptus trunks which Juanito had cut loose.

'Fine, Juanito, I think these'll do,' he said in a firm voice, bending down.

'Don't touch them!' Juanito hissed threateningly, drawing close to Jean.

'Why not? What do you mean to use them for, Juanito?' Jean asked politely.

'That's no business of yours. Leave me alone.'

His voice trembled with suppressed rage. Eric turned with an effort and looked sternly at Juanito. Suddenly Juanito lost all self-control and poured out a confused stream of words:

'I'm going to build my boat now whether you like it or not . . . I can't stand it any longer . . . do you hear . . . shut up, all of you . . . it's all over . . . we're dying slowly of thirst . . . and I who will live, live . . . don't you understand that . . . and it's all your fault . . . your fault—'

He pointed a quivering finger accusingly at Eric.

This was too much for me. Even if Juanito was suffering from temporary mental aberration, we could not go on treating him with consideration. I shouted, beside myself with rage:

'Hold your tongue, or you'll be sorry for it. Do you think you're the only person on board who wants to live? As far as I can understand, everyone of us is as keen as another to come through this adventure with a whole skin. But if we're to have a chance of getting through we must stick together. Anyone who goes off alone is lost at once.'

Eric joined in and, showing great patience, made several tactful attempts to calm Juanito. But reasonable argument no longer had any effect, for instead of listening he uttered fearful threats and began to brandish the axe furiously. Then suddenly he fell silent and vanished into the cabin looking scared. But this hardly made the situation any less serious. We held a ship's council at once, and to our great joy and relief Eric showed astonishing resolution and power of action. The following report which he drafted immediately afterwards, and which I here quote verbatim, describes what had happened:

At sea, on board Tahiti Nui II

Today, July 21, 1958, at 2 P.M. by local time, our position being 6° 46′ south by 147° 36′ west, I called together my deputy Alain Brun, Jean Pélissier and Hans Fischer to consider and take a decision on the following serious matter:

Juanito Bugueño, who has been causing us anxiety for some time past, has just declared that he 'has decided to build himself a raft and clear out'.

When I tried to make him understand that he could not always do just what he liked without regard to the well-being and safety of the rest of us, he threatened with an axe he had in his hand and cried menacingly that 'he would not let anyone try to prevent him from building a raft'.

These are the most important facts.

After discussing the matter we have decided unanimously:

(1) to let Juanito Bugueño build his raft on condition that he does not thereby diminish Tahiti Nui II's *already much reduced buoyancy;*

(2) whether he will or not, to compel our former comrade without hesitation or compassion to cast off—having first received his share of the provisions and water—as soon as his raft is completed.

I have read this report to Juanito Bugueño so that he shall not be ignorant of what we have decided.

Done in duplicate on board
E. de Bisschop
Captain

While Eric, exhausted by his immense exertions, was sinking once more into a profound trance, we others continued our occupations with as indifferent an air as possible. But we could not help casting now and then a compassionate glance towards the starboard side, where Juanito, wearing a happy smile, was nailing a few planks on to two spars about three feet long. These were evidently his oars. As soon as he had finished them he made a triangular frame of eucalyptus slats, and to judge from the numerous measurements which he took of two of our ten-gallon tanks it looked as if he intended to make a kind of raft. Evidently he had quite abandoned his ambitious plan of building a boat which would do four knots. That was always something to be thankful for. If he had persisted in it we should have been obliged to prevent him by force from taking timber which we could not spare without imperilling our own safety. Juanito worked hard and quickly, but of course that did not make his queer craft any more seaworthy. It could be at best a toy for a native child in a shallow lagoon. But we were still hundreds of miles from the nearest island with a lagoon, which moreover was on the windward side of *Tahiti Nui II,* and to attempt to get there with this toy raft was sheer suicide.

I felt strongly inclined to rush forward and shake Juanito till he realized how insanely he was behaving. But I refrained, for I knew in my inmost heart that the best solution for us all was to let him clear out. He had long ago passed the stage at which his eccentricity had taken such comparatively harmless forms as refusing to take watches or to be cook, and now he was undoubtedly a danger to our security. Cruel as it was, I suppressed all the brotherly compassion I felt for him and let him carry on.

Apparently pleased with his day, Juanito climbed up on to the roof late that night and curled up in his usual place, evidently quite unaware that Hans and I were lying there, a few inches away, oppressed and unhappy, staring up at the overclouded sky. (Jean was at the helm and Eric was still plunged in a deep trance.) In five minutes he was asleep. He was probably more dangerous to himself than to anyone else; nevertheless Jean, Hans and I agreed to keep an eye on him throughout our watches. I gradually dozed off and had horrible dreams of swarthy fellows paddling round on large bottles and only laughing contemptuously every time I begged them to let me have a little water. After a time one of my tormentors came ashore on the little island I thought I was sitting on, and began to shake me violently, bellowing something in one of my ears at the same time. I tried to free myself, but he would not let go of my shoulders. Not for a long time did I realize that I was dreaming no longer and that it was Hans who was trying to wake me. I felt that he was trying eagerly to tell me something, but in my drowsy state I could not hear what he was saying. Then I suddenly remembered the events of the previous day and was wide awake in an instant. What had Juanito been up to now? I looked round quickly and saw his curled up form in the same place as before. To judge by his quiet regular breathing he was still sound asleep.

'Don't you notice anything unusual?' asked Hans, holding out his hand.

I held out my hand. Several damp spots appeared on it at once. Soon the drops were falling quickly. There could no longer be any doubt. The longed-for miracle had come about at last. For the first time since we left Callao there was a good downpour of rain. I jumped up, meaning to spread out all our sails quickly so that no more precious drops might be lost, but Hans checked me and pointed with a little smile to a large canvas funnel which he had rigged up at the edge of the cabin roof. Under the funnel stood a saucepan. Hans was justifiably proud of his unusual handiness, and I was not sparing of my praises. While the rain continued to pour down, Hans, Jean and I rapidly hunted up all the empty casks, demijohns, saucepans and bottles which we had on board.

When we crawled up on to the roof again, clasping our varied collection of vessels in our arms, the saucepan under the canvas funnel was already full. Jean filled a cup and gave it to Eric, who emptied it slowly with a reverent expression and handed it back with the moving words:

'Thanks for the greatest and purest enjoyment of my life.'

Like Jean and Hans, I had more difficulty in restraining my eagerness and plunged almost the whole of my face into a saucepan and greedily swallowed several pints almost at a draught. I felt that the water was spreading into the farthest corners of my dried-up body, for my arms gradually became curiously heavy. At the same time my head became heavier and heavier, as if even my brain had sucked up some of the water. So it was not so strange as it sounds that only much later, when I was lying comfortably stretched out on my back with several vessels containing water within my reach, did I suddenly become aware of Juanito squatting beside me and drinking out of a bottle. He had probably been squatting there for a long time, for he was only taking a little sip now and then. When he saw that I had noticed him, he put down the bottle, smiled at me apologetically and said gently:

'Do you realize that it is God who sent this rain? He sent it to prevent me from doing a very stupid thing which would have cost me my life. The rain is a sign that God wants me to live.'

He seemed quiet and normal again. Shortly afterwards he crept over to Eric and begged with touching sincerity for forgiveness for his shameful behaviour. Of course, we were all more than delighted at the unexpectedly happy end to the tragic situation and forgave him absolutely. Juanito, radiant with joy, disappeared into the lower regions and came back with a bottle of Chilean brandy which he must have hidden away during our early period at sea, when he was still our cook. We came near falling on his neck for joy at the welcome gift of reconciliation, begging his pardon in our turn. A large glass of warming brandy was just what we needed, for we were wet through, our teeth chattered and we shivered in the bitter wind.

When the cloudburst stopped some hours later, just before daybreak, all our tanks were full, and a hasty estimate showed that we had all at once increased our water supply from three to about forty gallons. But we soon realized that we had had to pay a very high price for our delicious drinking water. Like ourselves, all our clothes, bundles, parcels and other things which surrounded us on the roof had absorbed great quantities of water and quickly became heavier. There was also the weight of the drinking water, which was nearly 400 lb. The inevitable result was that the top-heavy raft began to sway to and fro in the heavy sea. Our position became still worse when soon afterwards the wind died down and the raft suddenly ceased to answer her helm. As a result she quickly laid herself broadside on to the sea with an ominous splashing and heeled over so violently that the trunks on the port side became visible above water. We crawled over to the port side in alarm as quickly as we could, and, by leaning far out over the edge of the roof, we finally managed to prevent the raft from capsizing. Next moment, however, she began to sway slowly back in the opposite direction, and the only way to prevent a catastrophe was to crawl back again across the roof and create an equilibrium.

'Have you ever thought that there are yachtsmen who do balancing tricks like this every Sunday just for amusement?' Hans asked in a voice of sincere astonishment, when we were crossing the roof for the third or fourth time in quick succession.

Although we did not feel at all like joking, we could not help smiling. But it was not long before our faces were as gloomy as ever. Our situation was highly unpleasant, and the only gleam of light was that a week or so before, by a lucky inspiration, we had cut a hole in one corner of the roof and let Eric's bed down by eighteen inches or so, so that he came to rest in a narrow box in which he had just room to turn round. If he had still been on top of the roof like the rest of us he would inevitably have rolled into the sea and been drowned the first time the raft heeled over.

Quite understandably, however, I soon grew tired of thinking about what could have happened, and began instead to think all the harder about what we were to do to get ourselves out of the very real difficulty we were in. It was useless now to try to turn the raft round ninety degrees with the help of the oar, so that the stern was to the sea, as there was no wind to keep her in this position and give her stability. After a further half-hour of involuntary morning gymnastics I at last had an idea which I hastened to confide to Eric the next time I had to form a counterweight alongside him. My idea was founded upon an observation I thought I had made—namely, that the main reason why the raft took such a heavy list every time she rolled was that the water which was shut into the cabin by its weight accelerated the pendulum movement. The logical solution was obviously to cut away the walls of the cabin and give the waves free play.

Although I suspected that the wooden posts which supported the roof and ourselves might be weakened if we took away the walls, I thought that we ought to try this experiment. If it was really the case that we must choose between disappearing quickly and suddenly and doing so after prolonged torment, I decidedly preferred the first manner of death, and I supposed that all hands shared this view. Despite my eloquence my shipmates showed no great enthusiasm for my proposal, but on the other hand they showed no sign of wanting to hinder me, which was all I asked for. I therefore armed myself with the unfortunate ship's axe, which I had carefully hidden since Juanito's outbreak, and climbed down from the roof. Fortunately the walls consisted only of sheets of masonite, and I should not have had the least difficulty in smashing them under normal conditions.

But conditions on board *Tahiti Nui II* had for a long time been far from normal, and I had scarcely made a small hole on one side of the cabin when I had to scurry over to the opposite side in order not to be drawn down into the depths when the raft heeled over. To divert my thoughts into rather more pleasant channels I began to study the still quite legible messages of good wishes which well-meaning visitors had scribbled on the walls when the raft was being built at Constitucion. Most of them—even one which in martial style exhorted us to seek a hero's death rather than give up—left me quite cold. But when just after this I caught sight of an inscription in red chalk which ran: LUCKY BOYS TO GET SUCH A HOLIDAY TRIP, I grew angry and disposed of the rest of the masonite in double quick time.

To my own and my comrades' inexpressible relief, my guess proved right. The raft at once became so steady that we were able to stop our exhausting acrobatics. She became steadier still a few hours later, when our sails filled again. The wind was doubly welcome, for it was north-easterly and made it possible for us to steer down towards Vostok, where we knew that there was a gang of Tahitian labourers making copra for a Papeete firm. We knew because it was this firm which had bought the Chilean yacht on board which Juanito had been a mechanic when he made his first voyage to Tahiti, for the special purpose of carrying labourers, food supplies and copra between Tahiti and Vostok, Caroline and Flint.

If the wind was a blessing from the point of view of our equilibrium, it soon proved extremely damaging in another respect. The raft had no sooner become steerable again when several violent thuds told us that the white-crested waves which were now running unchecked right through our wall-less cabin were sweeping away what remained of our equipment. Even if we had been able to plunge down and save the most important things—which would certainly have been difficult in the dark—we had no room for them on the roof. So we did the next best thing: we slept, or pretended to sleep, when we were not keeping a watch.

Even when daylight came we could not ascertain the extent of the damage on account of the heavy sea. The raft now became livelier than ever, and the wind increased so rapidly in strength that we had to take in the sails in a hurry so that the fragile little platform on which we anxiously crowded together might not be forced down under water. Soon we were again compelled to move to and fro from one side of the roof to the other to counteract the rolling—certainly not as often as immediately after the cloudburst, but often enough to make these wearisome movements a torment. Also, it soon began to rain again, and this time we felt no desire whatever to shout aloud for joy.

Day after day, night after night, the stormy weather continued, and, with only a few interruptions, the pouring rain also. The raft, or rather the wreck which had once been a raft, rolled and lurched helplessly in the rough sea, without sails or steersman. Our strength and our will to live slowly disappeared, and for long periods we were completely numbed and indifferent to our fate. When I now look back on this terrible time I wonder if it was not really a good thing that the raft did roll, for if we had not maintained the warmth of our bodies by our enforced movements we should certainly all have got pneumonia. As for Eric, at least we prevented him from getting noticeably worse by rigging up a small tent and wringing out his clothes frequently.

On July 27th we were all convinced that the end was near. The sky was overcast as usual, and the howling wind whipped our naked shivering bodies pitilessly. As soon as our rags began to dry a little a squall of rain came and soaked them again. White foaming waves licked the edges of the roof and now and then, for a change, drenched us in a cascade of salt water. Hans alone broke the oppressive silence once, and that was to tell us, to our surprise, that he was going to change his profession and become a farmer on his return to Chile. He added dreamily:

'Think how jolly it will be to be able to sit down out in the middle of a field and let the earth run through one's fingers.'

It was not the first time that Hans had lightened our spirits with priceless remarks of this kind. Curiously enough he always seemed to be in a good humour, simply because, being so unpractical by nature and a regular landsman, he had still not really grasped the seriousness of our situation. He had often made remarks indicating that he regarded our disastrous voyage almost as a kind of scouts' exercise, with intentionally planned tests of endurance and handiness. Only a week or two before, for example, he had seriously reproached me with the monotony of life on board, just as if this had been our most serious problem and I had been able to do something about it. But this only made me like Hans the better and wish that all of us on board had had his humour.

At first we felt that the coming of night was an act of mercy, for at least we could then no longer see one another's miserable shapes. But before long we were so horribly cold that despite our weariness we had a fierce crawling race every time the raft heeled over. From this I should except not only poor Eric but also Juanito, who, incredible as it may seem, slept well. We left him in peace, for he had been queer again for the last few days. For the first time since the raft had begun to sink two months earlier we were in real danger, but it is indicative of my state of exhaustion that I felt no agony of mind or fear, but rather a happy relief at the thought that I might soon slip down and disappear for ever into the warm, soft sea.

Nevertheless, I continued almost automatically to cling fast to the platform, 10 feet wide and 13 feet long, which formed my entire world, and to my boundless astonishment not only I but all my shipmates were still alive when the eastern horizon began slowly to grow light. The sea was a trifle calmer, and the raft was no longer lurching quite so violently, but still we dared not lie down and sleep, although sleep was what we most longed for. Suddenly, without saying a word, Jean slipped down from the roof and disappeared. I was still so bemused that I did not get to the point of wondering what had become of him and if he would ever come back, and therefore did not react in any way till he reappeared over the edge of the roof clasping the gas cooker. Then at last I lent a hand, feeling rather ashamed of myself. We put the cooker into a deep suitcase in which it was nearly if not quite protected from the wind, and I helped him to find a packet of damp macaroni. Contrary to our expectations the gas cooker was still working, and soon we were all sitting with large plates of macaroni on our knees, swaying to and fro in time with the raft.

We had luckily escaped what seemed certain death at the last moment. But how long would our period of grace last? For there could be scarcely any doubt that it would be all up if another storm arose. If we wanted to save our lives—and after this good meal, I again wished to live—we had better do something quickly before it was too late. I could think as far as this, but then my brain came to a dead stop. I therefore appealed to my comrades for a bright idea, but they only stared dully out into space without answering. Obviously they were no cleverer than I. So only Eric remained. Surprisingly enough he was fully conscious and alert, and signed to me to come closer.

'We must increase our stability at all costs,' he began in an unusually firm and clear voice.

I made a deprecatory, impatient gesture. This was in itself quite excellent advice. But hadn't we already done everything in our power to make the raft steadier?

'I've been lying here a long time trying to imagine what a Polynesian would have done in our situation,' Eric continued unmoved. 'I've just found the solution. A Polynesian would try to make an outrigger.'

Eric was certainly right. If large canoes holding half-a-dozen men, such as I had often seen, could maintain their balance by means of a single slender tree trunk, it should certainly be possible to make a raft stable in the same way. My shipmates felt rather foolish and wondered why we had not hit upon this simple and admirable solution earlier. Without delay we set about the task with new energy. We had had enough sense to make fast the cut-down masts alongside the raft for future use, and now, much pleased with our foresight, we brought them up. While Juanito and Hans formed a counterweight, the only thing they were any good for—Juanito because he had gone to sleep again and Hans because he was so desperately unpractical—Jean and I pushed out two of the stumps on the windward side at a right angle to the longitudinal axis of the raft and tied them firmly with a couple of ropes' ends.

The next problem was to find a suitable float. The Polynesians make their outriggers of the light wood of the bread-fruit tree, but we had nothing of the kind on board. We thought for a time that one of the balsa trunks which we had pushed in under the cabin floor at Callao would serve our purpose, but unfortunately we could not get at them. For that matter, they were certainly too small and fragile. After racking our brain for a long time, we finally made a really fine float out of a eucalyptus trunk by making fast all our empty gas bottles under it.

The raft at once became noticeably steadier, and even when the wind freshened again towards evening she rolled so slightly that we only needed to change our positions very little at long intervals. Jean, Hans and I therefore divided the night into watches so that one of us could sleep while the other two by their own weight prevented the raft from capsizing. Although we did not get many hours' sleep, we had enough rest to be almost normally alert when the day dawned and the sun peeped out again on July 29th. Our spirits rose with the sun, and while our clothes and bedclothes dried quickly we stretched ourselves out and fully enjoyed the life-giving warmth. Even Juanito thawed to such a degree that a few hours later he helped us to cut rope lashings when we were taking the precaution of strengthening the outrigger, on whose durability our lives now really depended.

I was also able to take an observation at noon for the first time after a long interval. A quick look at the chart showed us that since July 25th we had drifted west-northwest, i.e., away from the three copra islands, Vostok, Caroline and Flint. The nearest island in the direction in which we were drifting was another atoll, Starbuck. But it was about 400 miles away, and we knew from sad experience how capricious the wind could be, so we had no great hope of reaching it. For the moment we were a good deal more interested in a dolphin which Jean declared that he had seen in our wake keeping company in brotherly fashion with the untiring brown shark. Before we could jump down from the roof and assure ourselves with our own eyes that Jean was not pulling our legs, he had grasped his spear-gun, jumped in quickly and harpooned the dolphin at the first shot.

But no pleasure lasts for ever, and least of all when one is on board a drifting wreck. We were therefore not greatly astonished when, in the middle of our banquet, Eric pointed out that the raft had sunk at least four inches during the recent storms. We all had our different tests for deciding how deep the raft lay, and it did not take us long to establish that unfortunately Eric was right. Our delight at having stabilized the raft so well and at having water and food for at least another month was therefore considerably damped, for in the long run our fate depended, of course, entirely on how long the raft could keep afloat. It was clear that the only thing we could do to lighten the raft was to throw as much as possible overboard. But this was far from simple to carry out. We had thrown away a great deal of equipment a long time ago, and since then had uncritically assumed that all the things we had kept were absolutely indispensable. Obviously we must modify our claims.

We looked round us appraisingly. There was not much more on the roof than our bedclothes, the many water tanks, what remained of our provisions and the large wireless set. A net had been stretched between two posts on the after-deck, and suspended in it were five suitcases containing our clothes, books, and other personal belongings. Inside the cabin a quantity of oceanographic apparatus and cameras were still hanging from the roof, and on both sides of the cabin Jean's heavy cases with many thousands of samples of sea water and plankton must still exist somewhere in more than three feet of water. Finally we had a heavy anchor with a chain.

There was no doubt that we could dispense with all these things except the food supplies and the water without lethal consequences. The suitcases with our personal belongings weighed very little, so we might as well keep them for the present, especially as it would certainly be bad for our morale to get rid of the last little things which reminded us of our homes and families. The heaviest objects were of course Jean's eight cases of plankton and water samples, the most important result of the oceanographical studies he had been carrying on for more than half a year. Perhaps he would find it easier to part with them if we began with something else. No sooner said than done. Splash! there went the anchor. Splash! the long chain followed it. After a few minutes of melancholy hesitation Jean untied the rope which held the nearest case fast, and let the waves wash the case away. To prevent him from changing his mind we quickly helped him to free the raft of the remaining cases. Then we waded into the open cabin, where the sea was running high as usual, and cleared everything out. Then, secure in the knowledge that we had done all that was in our power to lighten the raft, we climbed up on to the roof again to see if our exertions had produced the desired result (which was by no means the case). As soon as Eric caught sight of us he pointed silently at the big wireless transmitter and the engine and nodded meaningly in the direction of the sea.

Our actions, as everyone knows, are often determined by pure wishful thinking, and this had certainly been the case with us when we had not brought ourselves to to get rid of the wireless transmitter as part of our first clearing up. Simply because we so earnestly wished for it to function, we had believed that one fine day it really would. Indeed, we were so dominated by our faith that we refused to throw the transmitter into the sea without making a last attempt to call for help. So that same evening we brought out three-quarters of a gallon of petrol which was all we had left, and started the engine. For the first time since our trial transmission in Callao harbour the pointers on all the dials worked. I seized the microphone trembling with excitement, and began to call expectantly:

'SOS, SOS, here *Tahiti Nui II*. We are sinking, SOS, SOS . . .'

We thought there was a better chance of our despairing SOS being picked up if we spread out the transmissions, so we stopped the engine after two periods of ten minutes and repeated them two evenings later. When our petrol ran out on the third evening there was still no reply. But of course that did not mean that no one had heard us, and we tried hard to delude one another as we slowly pushed the transmitter and engine to the edge of the deck and saw them disappear into the sea. The only superfluous things which now remained on board were the suitcases and ourselves.

Chapter 7

NEW RAFT, NEW HOPE

Our compulsory sacrifices did not avail us for long, for only two days later the raft began to sink again. To attempt to steer her was of course now out of the question, nor would she carry the least scrap of sail. Although she was thus a complete wreck we did as much as twenty-five miles a day with the kindly aid (we supposed) of a westerly ocean current. The strong favouring wind too was unusually helpful, and was driving us straight towards Starbuck. As the pencil line which marked our route on the chart gradually approached the island, we slowly recovered hope and courage.

On August 6th we had still only 250 miles to cover, and our course was still the same. But we saw clearly that the wind had only to change a few degrees and we should miss our insignificant goal, which was no bigger on the chart than a pin's head. It was, moreover, far from certain that the raft would remain afloat for another ten days, and this, according to our careful estimates, was roughly the time we should take to reach Starbuck. As I understood the situation, the moment had come to try to build a craft in which to make our escape. Eric, whom of course I consulted, as always before I took any important decision, was unreservedly of the same opinion.

When, however, I expressed my views to my other comrades they stared at me in speechless astonishment for a long time, and then told me in sharp language that I had impudently pinched their idea, and that it was chiefly my fault that they had not been able to carry it out before. But their attitude gradually altered: they began to praise me rather patronizingly for having at last changed my mind for the better, and several times they were even good-natured enough to give me a lot of idiotic pieces of advice.

Of course, I should have been fully justified in telling them that to set off quite at random, without a plan, as they had wanted to do, and undertaking a short sail under particularly favorable conditions, as I proposed, were not at all the same thing. But their behaviour showed that it would be hopeless to try to make them see this important difference, and of course the main thing was that on the whole we were agreed and would help one another to carry out our daring plan. I therefore turned the conversation on to our first and most important problem—what kind of craft we were to build. It was not long before we were all talking at once in our eagerness to convince one another of the excellence of our different types of boat and raft.

When Eric at last got a word in edgeways, he only asked us briefly to look at a sketch he had made. At the first glance we were unwillingly compelled to admit that all our own ideas were clumsy monstrosities beside Eric's well-conceived design of a craft which should properly have been called an outrigger raft.

As on several previous occasions during his long life as a seaman and boat-builder, Eric had on this occasion obtained his inspiration from a primitive model, for his remarkable creation had two outriggers like a Melanesian canoe. But if his source of inspiration was primitive, the material which Eric meant to use for the building was correspondingly modern. It consisted of empty water containers (which were presumably still in their places below decks), arranged in three rows with the larger ones in the middle and the smaller ones on both sides as stabilizing floats. Each row of tanks was held together by a wooden frame, and stout cross-beams were stretched across the three rows of tanks to keep them in place. On top of the cross-beams there was a rectangular deck of masonite plates. It really seemed that Eric had succeeded in combining in the same vessel the lightness and stability of an outrigger canoe and the spaciousness of a raft.

But how were we actually placed? We looked at Eric's sketch rather more closely and made a rapid inventory of our supply of materials and tools. If we omitted the rusty galvanized iron tanks from Constitucion, which it

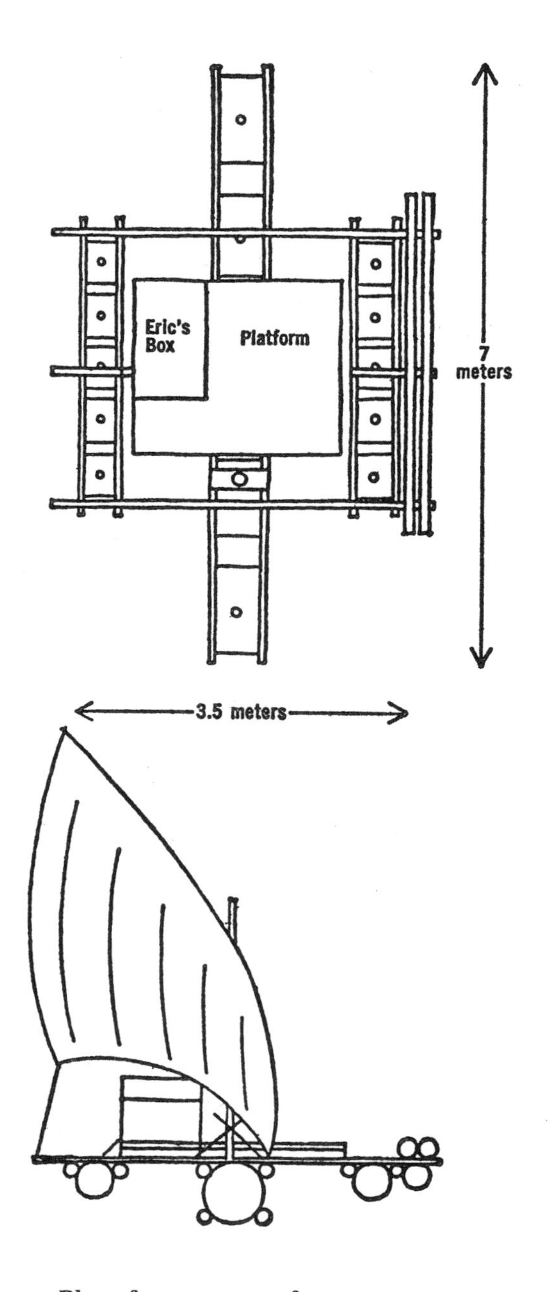

Plan of emergency raft TAHITI NUI III
built on the final stage of the voyage to Polynesia

would certainly be wisest to do, we should have only the five 40-gallon and the ten 10-gallon tanks, all of aluminium, which we had shipped at Callao. For a long time we doubted whether these would be enough, but after long calculation we came to the reassuring conclusion that the vessel would in fact be strong enough to carry us.

The supply of timber also seemed very scanty. To begin with we required six long slats and a still uncertain number of short ones to make frames round the rows of tanks. We also wanted three or four strong beams to hold the three rows together. And finally we had to find suitable spars for a mast and a steering oar. But we ought to be able to manage if we saved, patched and spliced as hard as we could. Further, as a last expedient, we could always try to get a little extra timber by carefully dismantling *Tahiti Nui II*.

The next problem was how to join together the various sticks and scraps of wood. There were not more than fifty nails in our tool-box, and most of them were rusty and bent. But we hoped optimistically that we might be able to pull out some of the nails which we saw here and there in the cabin roof without any disastrous consequences, and to use ropes when this limited supply came to an end. For that matter it would certainly be better in all circumstances to lash together all the larger spars. Fortunately we had an unusually large coil of rope, given us by a kindly Chilean sea captain.

When our plans had reached this stage we remembered, not without some anxiety, that our only tools were a sheath-knife, a blunt axe, a file and a hammer. But we consoled ourselves with the thought that if, as the proverb says, necessity is really the mother of invention, we should be the most inventive and original-minded people in the southern hemisphere. We were well aware that every minute was valuable, so we cheerfully decided to start building the boat at once. An impatient gesture from Eric, who seemed to have been listening attentively to our discussion, although he had had his eyes shut all the time, checked us abruptly.

'Wait a minute,' he said in a complaining voice. 'Strictly speaking, you ought to complete our new boat before you take away the tanks. But of course she can't be completed without these same tanks.

'So if we're not to fall into the sea between two useless rafts you must do your building by stages. First complete the wooden frame of the outrigger raft. Then take up the ten small 10-gallon tanks, fasten them in their places under the outriggers, and launch the half-finished raft. If we move over to her at once and take with us as much of our gear as we can, there's a good prospect of No. 2 remaining afloat long enough for you to be able to salvage the big tanks and complete No. 3. I hope you understand that the quicker you work the better chance of success you have. One more point. Whatever you do, don't take the outrigger away till the very last moment, for without it *Tahiti Nui II* will capsize at once.'

We began to clear up the after-deck, where we meant to do our building, in a considerably more serious frame of mind. The clearing up was an easy job, for the only things left on the after-deck were the net and the cases which held our personal belongings. The cases were an unnecessary dead weight which we should be obliged to get rid of sooner or later, so we firmly decided not to postpone the inevitable sacrifice for sentimental reasons. Our real feelings may be judged from the fact that we did not fling the cases overboard at once, but opened them and reluctantly threw away our treasured possessions one by one. A long trail of books, shirts and smart shore-going clothes were soon bobbing about in our wake to the great delight of our faithful shark. Juanito, however, true to his habit of always doing the opposite of what the rest of us did, shut his case again in a few minutes and declared emphatically that he meant to keep all his clothes. His reason, which we found a little far-fetched, was that he did not want to return to Chile stark naked. That Juanito should keep his clothes was not in itself of any consequence, but I feared that this episode would soon be followed by others more serious. I therefore took him aside and warned him that I would not take him on board our escape craft if he did not behave properly. With touching eagerness he at once promised both to help build the craft and take watches like the rest of us and to do whatever I wished—if only he might keep his clothes. I was anxious to give him yet another chance, so I agreed.

The first visible result of Juanito's sudden conversion was that soon afterwards he proposed of his own accord that we should take to pieces the three-cornered 'lifeboat' which had been hanging on the starboard side since his temporary mental aberration a fortnight before. But this was only a beginning, for he again made great efforts to be useful when, immediately afterwards, we began to make the wooden frames for the tanks. This proved more difficult than we had expected on account of the violent waves which threatened again and again to wash us away, as well as our precious wood and our irreplaceable tools. When, to our great annoyance, the sun sank swiftly in the west we had completed two frames, which was quite a good performance in the circumstances. Well satisfied with our day we carefully secured the frames and stretched ourselves out on the cabin roof dead-tired.

We were on our legs again immediately after sunrise on August 7th, fresh and well-rested after ten hours of undisturbed sleep. We had the previous day disposed of all former bowsprits, stanchions and other superfluous wood, which had been lashed fast at different places on the raft. Our first problem, therefore, was how we could produce yet a few more slender spars for the last frame and a few beams strong enough to serve as connecting links between the three floats. After great exertions and many cold drinks we at last succeeded in loosening a sufficient number of the slats on which the long vanished willow deck had rested. These were to complete the last frame.

While we were putting the frame together I was thinking hard about the next stage in our building. The only beams on board of any size were four masts, two of which were serving as outrigger booms on the port side and two were still forming a double mast on the fore-deck. We needed them all, but to take away the stabilizing outrigger booms at this early stage was certainly dangerous. On the other hand, the double mast on the fore-deck no longer fulfilled any function since the raft had become quite unsteerable, and we should therefore be able to cut it down without loss. With the two stumps of masts obtained in this way we could provisionally join together our escape raft till we were ready to leave *Tahiti Nui II* and it was at last possible to take away the outrigger booms without risk and reinforce No. 3's framework with them. It was certainly not the ideal way of doing things, but we had no other choice. My shipmates fortunately took the same view as I did and helped me to cut down the double mast. The result was doubly satisfactory, for not only did we get a couple of first-class cross-beams, but *Tahiti Nui II* became steadier at once.

According to Eric's carefully organized working programme we ought to fix the cross-beams before we made fast the 10-gallon tanks under the side frames. But we soon became convinced that it would be easier to do the opposite, and Eric rapidly conceded that we were right. Juanito at once offered, with touching eagerness, to dive down and bring up the 10-gallon tanks, which were firmly wedged into the raft's bottom about five feet under water. We thought he still owed us a really good turn for his earlier behaviour and therefore accepted his offer without protest. With a broad grin Juanito put on one of Jean's diving masks and disappeared into the waves.

While Jean, Hans and I were hurriedly arranging a number of lashings we cast curious eyes towards the spot at which he reappeared from time to time, blowing hard, to take breath for a new attack on the obviously recalcitrant tanks. At last we could control ourselves no longer, but splashed our way over to him to see what was wrong.

'I've got the first tank loose, but it's still just where it was,' said Juanito, looking unhappy.

This could mean only one thing—that the tank was full of water. We helped him to lift it up, expecting the worst; and we were right, for the water poured away from a hole in its side. Of course it was not rusty, for it was made of aluminium, but nevertheless, for some reason we could not guess, there was a hole in it as big as a man's little finger. A sudden idea flashed into my mind. Were we, perhaps, sinking simply because all the tanks were full of water? If so it would be enough to throw the unwanted ballast overboard and, hey presto! the raft would recover her buoyancy. I eagerly helped Juanito to loosen the next tank. It rose to the surface at once and floated like a cork. I began once more to incline to my previous view, that we were sinking not because of but in spite of the tanks. Trembling all over with excitement, I dived down and cut the rope which held the next tank. This one too floated up at once: likewise the next, and the next, and the next. I felt a good deal easier, but not quite easy, in my mind. Some of the remaining tanks might be damaged, and if we were compelled to make do with a smaller number than we had counted on, our escape craft would presumably not be strong enough to bear us.

It grew dark before we could bring up any more, and so we were obliged to break off our work at the, so far, most critical stage in the creation of *Tahiti Nui III*. To counteract the rolling, which had now become heavier, we lashed a centreboard on to the outrigger, which at once had the intended effect.

Still feeling rather uneasy, we quickly fished up the remaining 10-gallon tanks during the early morning hours of August 8th. They were all undamaged, and even with unlimited resources at our disposal we could certainly have found no better floats. We could even use the one damaged tank, which immediately solved all problems of equilibrium. Lashing the tanks to their frames with sliding knots was a comparatively quick job, and we were soon ready for the next task, which consisted in making fast the cross-beams, i.e., the former masts, between the two floats which had just been completed. This work, simple enough in itself, was made extremely difficult because the beams were many feet longer than the after-deck. We were therefore obliged to jump into the sea, which was still very rough, to prevent the rows of tanks from being swept away, and lash it firmly to the cross-beams, holding on all the time.

In such conditions the work was bound to be exasperatingly slow, and when at last we had hauled taut the last knot it was unfortunately too late to launch our queer creation. Nevertheless Juanito suddenly appeared with a bottle of brandy, but we were glad to find that it was by no means intended for the christening of No. 3, as we had thought at first, but for reviving our somewhat numbed vitality. Where Juanito had hidden this last bottle was a riddle to us all, but we had long ago lost all desire to try to solve Juanito's riddles (the greatest of which was undoubtedly his own personality), so we just grinned cheerfully and held out our cups to receive what seemed to us a most well-deserved reward for our good day's work. In our high spirits and cheerful mood—to which the brandy had really contributed very little—we all believed firmly that it was our last evening, or at the most our last evening but one, on board *Tahiti Nui II*.

As so often before, our apparently so well-grounded optimism was completely shattered, and that very night the wind shifted from south-east to north-east and gradually increased in strength. So instead of being able to launch and complete No. 3 on August 9th, as we hoped, we had to cling to the roof all day in complete inactivity. Although the waves played ball with the frames and tanks aft in an alarming manner, all our lashings and nailings held surprisingly well. On the other hand, both the rope with which she was made fast to the after-deck and the lashings of the outrigger booms seemed to be giving way, and although we had not the least desire to leave our comparatively safe places we climbed cautiously down from the roof and at last succeeded in strengthening the lashings after a most unpleasant balancing act. Encouraged by this success, we tried with astonishingly good results to persuade ourselves and each other that the wind would drop towards evening.

But the only thing that happened when dusk fell was that a large white sea-bird came fluttering wearily over the sea and settled on No. 3. We regarded this as an evil omen, and our judgment was proved right with terrifying speed. Compared with the roaring storm which soon afterwards flung itself upon us with unbridled fury, the strong north-easter of the previous day was but a gentle breath of trade wind. The impenetrable darkness and the howling wind quite blinded and deafened us, while the uninterrupted vibration of the roof-platform on which we lay reminded us only too clearly of the strain to which the outrigger booms and our half-finished escape craft were subjected.

It was particularly nasty when the waves lifted No. 3 right up and bumped her against the cabin stanchions so that the roof-platform shook for minutes on end like a house of cards on the point of collapse, and each time this happened we froze to the marrow. We knew only too well that we should soon be finished if the outrigger booms went or our escape craft was washed away by the raging waves. But we saw just as clearly that we should be washed away at once if we tried to leave the roof to inspect the lashings. Although our fate was about to be decided, the only thing we could do was to hope that the Polynesian sea-god Taaroa, upon whom Eric declared that he had called with success on several earlier occasions, would help us again this time.

Whether it was due to Taaroa's intervention, or to someone on board having sent up a prayer to another and mightier God, when daylight came at last at about six on the morning of August 10th the gale had so far moderated that we were able to slip down and inspect No. 3. Incomprehensibly, she had not suffered any serious damage. Immediately afterwards the white sea-bird rose and flew away, which of course we took as a sign that the storm was over. Indeed, the wind fell gradually, but unfortunately it was still north-easterly, which gave us too southerly a course. It was therefore high time that we completed No. 3, for only if we quickly exchanged our helpless wreck for a navigable craft could we have any chance now of reaching Starbuck.

No. 3 still had no middle float, but before we set about making one from the five large forty-gallon tanks, which were still under No. 2's flooded deck, we ought, according to our programme, to launch her. The object of this was, of course, to prevent No. 3 from being drawn down into the depths if No. 2 should sink suddenly when the big tanks were removed. If such a disaster occurred we could then easily save ourselves by swimming across to No. 3. Or, to be more correct, we could all do it but Eric. Of course we saw that in Eric's bad state of health he must at all costs be prevented from getting wet, and we therefore decided to put him on board No. 3 before we took up the tanks.

No. 3, however, consisted so far only of the two side floats held together by just a few cross-beams, so if we wanted to put this excellent plan into execution we should first have to make her rather more habitable. We did this by pulling a few dozen nails out of the roof platform and constructing an oblong box of planks and masonite. This box we then made fast to the port side of No. 3. This delicate carpentry work, however, took an inordinately long time, and it was not until two in the afternoon that Eric was at last established in his box.

Having achieved that much, we caught hold of No. 3 and shoved till our backs were near breaking. But it was not long before we prudently checked ourselves. The sea was still very high, and we were all afraid of the outrigger raft capsizing as soon as we let go. For safety's sake, therefore, we changed our tactics and lifted Eric out before making another attempt. It was still hard work, and several times we were alarmingly near disaster, but finally No. 3 slid into the water right way up. She floated uncommonly well, but pitched a good deal worse than No. 2. But that did not worry us excessively, for we were convinced that a steadying cargo was all she needed. We hauled No. 3 in quickly with the aid of a rope, and while Juanito and I held on tight, Jean and Hans together lifted Eric over and laid him down in the box. We also passed over in quick succession a sextant, the one usable wireless receiver, some nautical books and the greater part of our food supplies and our drinking water.

As Eric was completely helpless and many unforeseen accidents might happen, I asked Jean to keep him company. Then we gave No. 3 sixty feet of rope and let her go. But she had hardly gone a few yards when she came back with the wind and began to bump against our stern planks. It was futile to push her away, for she came back again and again as obstinately as a duckling afraid to leave its mother. At Eric's suggestion we hoisted a sail the size of a towel on board No. 3 and let out another thirty feet of rope, and the result was unexpectedly good; indeed she was now trying to sail away from us.

It was now three o'clock, and we therefore went to work without delay on the big forty-gallon tanks. The first one we loosened was full of water, but we were now hardened against such mishaps, and without losing any time in gloomy reflections we quickly took up the four remaining tanks—all in first-class condition. To our surprise and pleasure *Tahiti Nui II* sank only about four inches deeper. Nevertheless, to avoid any further collisions between the two craft we did not fasten them alongside one another but swam over to No. 3 with the tanks one by one and, with great trouble, made them fast under the middle frame. Every swim of thirty yards there and back took much time, and we were only just able to finish this tiring work before darkness fell.

As both our vessels were almost equally unsteady, we divided the crew between them, Eric and Jean spending the night on board No. 3 and Juanito, Hans and I on board No. 2. Unlike my two comrades, I slept extremely badly, and each time I awoke I was irresistibly driven to crawl to the edge of the roof and feel whether we still had No. 3 in tow. To be quite honest I will not deny that my uneasiness was caused by consideration for my own safety, for it would have been as fatal to me and my snoring comrades as to Eric and Jean if the worn rope had parted.

We began Monday, August 11th, by discussing how we could complete No. 3 in the shortest possible time. Our proud creation still lacked deck, mast, steering oar and additional cross-beams. But still we firmly believed that it would be possible to start our sail some time towards the end of the afternoon, if we only organized the work properly and put our backs into it. We were convinced that the storm had cleared the air for a long time ahead, and so, in making our plans, we quite ignored the possibility that the weather might worsen. This soon proved to have been a great mistake, for the sky slowly darkened again and the sea grew rougher and rougher.

Neither Juanito, who had been given the task of nailing down a deck of masonite plates, nor Eric and I, who were trying to make a steering oar, were troubled to any extent by the motion as we crawled about on the pitching No. 3. But poor Jean and Hans, to whose lot it had fallen to loosen as much wood as possible from No. 2 and swim across with it to No. 3, fought an uneven battle with the waves. For some unexplained reason, too, the sea that day was full of unpleasantly inquisitive sharks, which of course made their thankless task still more difficult. But they stubbornly refused to give in and, like the rest of us, continued against all reason to hope that No. 3 would be ready before evening.

But when darkness fell our escape craft still had no mast and, far more serious, we had not been able to reinforce her straining frame with No. 2's outrigger booms. We were therefore compelled, little as we liked it, once again to postpone our departure. As I ought to have realized would happen, those two archenemies, Eric and Jean, had been unable to get along together the previous night alone on board No. 3. So this time I asked Jean to stay on board No. 2 along with his trusty chum Hans, and I stretched myself out between Eric and Juanito on board No. 3.

I at once made two depressing discoveries, which had escaped me earlier in the day. First, the tank floats lay much deeper than we had estimated, which was the more disturbing in that we had nothing like a full cargo and crew on board. Secondly, I distinctly felt the big tanks in the central frame moving violently each time the outrigger raft climbed up on to a crest or slid down into the trough of a wave. I took counsel with the alert Eric, and we quickly agreed that it would be too risky to entrust our lives to No. 3 without first trying to reinforce her and increase her buoyancy.

The only way in which we could make No. 3 carry a rather heavier weight was to add those of the galvanized iron drums from Constitucion which were still intact. So as soon as it grew light on the morning of August 12th we began, in a depressed mood, to take them up from their places on No. 2's fore-deck. Three of them had rusted to pieces, but the other three were still usable, and we hastened to lash them fast in three of the outrigger's four corners. In the fourth and last corner we placed, for the sake of equilibrium, an untidy-looking but very strong float, made of all our empty demijohns fastened together in a large bundle. Then we immediately set to work to make a further frame from the wood which Jean and Hans had broken loose the day before. After scratching our heads over it for a long time, we had come to the conclusion that the best way to keep the large tanks of the central float in place was to put an extra frame under them so that they were held fast between it and the first frame on the upper side. Our calculation proved correct, for the tanks immediately ceased their irregular movement, with consequent strain on the lashings. The weather gradually improved and the sea grew calmer, which made these unforeseen tasks easier; nevertheless, they took a whole day. If we had managed to complete the outrigger raft we should certainly not have taken too tragic a view of the delay, but unfortunately, when the sun suddenly set, we had not yet been able to move the outrigger booms from No. 2 to No. 3. We felt downcast and irritable as we gazed out over the sea, still illuminated by a few lingering shafts of light.

A whole week had now passed since we had begun with high hopes to build our raft, and my noon observation had shown that we were less than a hundred miles from Starbuck; yet we were a good way south of the latitude in which the island lay, and with every hour that passed the north-easterly wind increased the angle between our desired and our actual course. After a careful study of the chart Eric said, as calmly as if he had been looking at a time-table to see what train he was to take:

'It's already too late to get to Starbuck. Let us set a

course for Penrhyn instead as soon as we are ready to leave tomorrow.'

I glanced quickly at the chart and saw that Penrhyn lay about 225 miles south-west of our position. There was no doubt that we had an infinitely better prospect of reaching this island than Starbuck, and I could not help being surprised and annoyed at not having perceived this obvious truth long before. But before I could express my agreement Jean and Hans began to attack Eric fiercely for his changeableness, stupidity, irresponsibility and a number of other disagreeable characteristics with which they saddled him. When at last they paused for a moment I tried as tactfully as possible to convince them that Eric was right, but it was of no avail, and the longer our argument continued the more bitter and violent it became.

Curiously enough, Juanito obviously found it hard to decide which side to take, for he never opened his mouth, but that was the only consolation I had. Our safety depended, now more than ever, on agreeing and co-operating fully, and if, for example, Jean and Hans refused to take watches the end would be disaster for us all. It was impossible to divide us into two groups, for all the usable material had gone to the building of our outrigger raft. So when we saw how fanatically determined Jean and Hans were to have their way, Eric and I at last reluctantly agreed first to make an attempt to reach Starbuck.

'But you must promise to let Alain and me set our course in future, if by any chance we should be unlucky enough to miss Starbuck,' added Eric.

Jean and Hans solemnly promised this without noticing Eric's sarcastic tone, and they must have found this easy enough, for there seemed to be no limit to their childish faith in a speedy end to all our difficulties. We parted in a depressed mood and soon fell asleep.

We removed the outrigger booms as soon as we had drunk our usual morning coffee on August 13th. The rolling increased quickly, but the expected catastrophe did not take place, no doubt because the sea was surprisingly calm. I therefore left Jean, Hans and Juanito on board No. 2 to recover the last pieces of timber and myself returned to No. 3 to cut out a sail under Eric's supervision. My crew-mates had already floated several pieces across, lying on their stomachs on them, when I suddenly heard a piercing yell from No. 2. The yelling came from Jean and Juanito, and when they had succeeded in attracting my attention they pointed to Hans, who was pushing a big outrigger boom in front of him in the water some twenty yards farther away. My first thought was that he had been attacked by a shark. But no triangular fins were to be seen anywhere, and Hans himself was grinning cheerfully and waving his hand reassuringly. Not till I watched him in bewilderment for a long time did I at last realize what was wrong. Instead of approaching No. 3, as he evidently seemed to think he was doing, he was slowly but surely drifting away from her. The reason was very simple. Although the wind was rather weak, the rafts, due to their comparatively large structures above water, drifted much faster than the completely submerged boom, which in any case was too big for Hans to handle alone.

I quickly searched through all bundles and boxes on board No. 3 to see if our last coil of rope was on board. But of course it was not. Fortunately, however, Jean had the same idea as myself, and hastily made fast one end of the rope which was still on board No. 2 round his waist and the other end round a stanchion. As soon as he had finished his preparations he threw himself into the sea. Strange to say, Hans did not seem yet to have realized that the gap was widening, for he waved reassuringly to Jean and a few seconds later calmly laid himself across the boom to draw breath for a while.

Jean reached Hans just before the rope came to an end and his own strength gave out. As the boom was at least as valuable as Hans's life, and Jean had his work cut out to persuade Hans that he needed saving, I jumped in and helped in the rescue. Not until we had sworn that he was really on his way back to South America, and described in detail how unpleasant it could be to float about on a log quite alone in the middle of the Pacific, did Hans reluctantly begin to show some gratitude. After this tragicomic incident we took great care to make fast to a lifeline all the wood with which we swam over from one raft to the other. The last object we took on board No. 3 was the wooden Polynesian image which we had had with us on the outward voyage on *Tahiti Nui I* and by a lucky chance had been able to save from our first shipwreck near the Juan Fernandez islands.

To our inexpressible relief we at last completed No. 3 in time to make a start before dusk. None the less, we postponed our departure till next day, as we wanted to be absolutely sure that our new raft was seaworthy before we cut the line which connected us with No. 2 and the still quite considerable amount of repair material on board her. After we had taken away the outrigger it was positively dangerous to remain on board No. 2, and the only thing regarding her fate which we could not predict with certainty was whether she would capsize before she sank or sink before she capsized. For the first time, therefore, we all clambered on board No. 3 for the night.

Just to find room for us all on the little deck platform, which measured only five feet by six feet six inches and was almost entirely hidden by all our boxes, sacks and bundles, was a difficult problem. Unable to find any other solution, we finally lay down on top of all the equipment and pressed ourselves together like sardines. Even worse was that the raft lay so deep that the waves licked the underside of the thin deck. I estimated our freeboard at a foot, which undeniably was the lowest possible.

These new trials naturally aggravated our irritability and nervous tension, and we bickered ceaselessly over the most absurd things. Eric was the only one who kept silent, but it was clear from his angry snortings that he heard every word of our petty quarrels and strongly condemned our behaviour. None the less I was startled when, towards midnight, he announced that he was through with us and would rather be left behind on board our old, sinking raft. At first I took him to mean that he was voluntarily seeking death solely because he could no longer put up with these occasional unpleasantnesses, which were really extremely trivial, and I tried to appeal to his reason and make him see how precipitate his decision was.

But when Eric refused to see reason I began to wonder whether there was not some other and weightier reason for his stubbornness. More than once during the hardships and sufferings of the last few months he had confessed to me that he was dead tired and could not think of any better end for an old sailor than to find eternal peace and quiet in the sea which alone had given purpose and meaning to his life. Could it be, too, that he wanted to disappear just at this moment to make the outrigger raft lighter, give us more room and so assist our escape?

I felt that only the most drastic arguments would have any effect, and declared that I would stay behind with him if he persisted in his resolve. He gave way at last, slowly and reluctantly.

During the night of August 13th–14th an almost dead calm set in. When, the following morning, we saw the long, gentle swell we thought we might as well continue to use No. 2 as a drogue—which was now all that she was good for—and complete our last preparations in peace and quiet while waiting for a wind. The first thing we did was to tidy up. By stowing the sextant, provisions and nautical books into Eric's box, and lashing the water tanks firmly to the outriggers, we succeeded in making room enough on deck for two of us at a time to stretch ourselves out in something like comfort. As we reckoned that one of us would always have to stand aft and steer, all that was needed was to find one more place, and seeing no other way out, I offered to sleep on the top of Eric's box when not on watch.

After that we tried to ship the mast, which proved to be a good deal more difficult than we had expected on account of the slippery aluminium tanks on which it stood. But gradually we got it shipped according to plan, at an angle of 75 degrees, in Polynesian style.

Then we paid a sentimental farewell visit to No. 2, which was now exactly like a submarine ready to dive.

When we crawled on board No. 3 again the sea was rippled by the first capful of wind, and to the general delight we agreed to cast off at once. We had been stupid enough, however, not to ask Eric's advice, so it was with justified impatience that he said, rather cuttingly:

'You silly mutts, you've forgotten to make a centreboard. I think you might have learnt by this time that a raft must have a centreboard if one's going to steer it. But don't use any of No. 2's centreboards: they're too heavy.'

Looking rather foolish, we hurriedly set to work to make a small centreboard of wooden spars and slabs of masonite and lashed it under the middle float as firmly as we could. While occupied with this tricky piece of work we did not keep a proper lookout, and suddenly the rafts came into collision with a violent crash. No. 3 had not suffered any visible damage, but it was far from certain that it would stand any more collisions of the kind, so when the next breeze came racing along the sea's surface a little later we cast off quickly and set sail. The breeze lasted just long enough to fill the sails, and we moved off slowly with Juanito grinning cheerfully at the steering oar.

Although *Tahiti Nui II,* once so pretty, had long been only a pitiable wreck, and we ought simply to be thankful that we had escaped from her alive, we followed her with melancholy looks till she disappeared below the horizon. Perhaps it was really not so strange that we had a certain feeling of sorrow, for we had spent 180 eventful days aboard her since we had left Constitucion.

Our outrigger raft sailed better than we had expected, but of course she could tack against the wind no more than her predecessor. The question which overshadowed everything else was, therefore, how many degrees we could diverge from the direction of the wind. By towing a short slat of wood in our wake we could get a good idea of our drift, and it proved, as I had expected, that this was much too great for us to be able to reach Starbuck with the north-easterly wind that still prevailed. Juanito had enough sea experience to realize this, but both Jean and Hans stubbornly refused to believe the evidence of their own eyes, and to judge from their talk they really seemed to think it was my fault that we could not steer straight for the island.

As early as noon on August 15th, when my observations showed that we were 70 miles south-east of Starbuck, I wanted to alter course and run down towards Penrhyn at once with the aid of the prevailing north-easterly wind. Jean and Hans, however, put forward the ridiculous argument that the wind might suddenly change, and insisted in such threatening language that we should do our utmost to reach Starbuck that I finally refrained from carrying out my intention. An inevitable result of this insane navigation was that just twenty-four hours later we sailed past Starbuck as much as 29 miles to the south.

When Jean and Hans, after staring mistrustfully at my calculations for a long time, at last realized that we had missed the island badly they were absolutely desperate. Although we others had not shared our comrades' vain hopes, we could not help feeling pretty depressed ourselves, for beyond Starbuck there were only a few equally insignificant coral islands and beyond these only empty sea as far as Samoa, which from a navigator's point of view was far from an ideal objective.

The only thing we knew for certain about Starbuck at that time was that in the position indicated on the chart there was a piece of solid ground which would not suddenly vanish under our feet, but that was more than enough for us. When, after our rescue, I returned to Tahiti I became rather more curious and several times asked some of the most experienced schooner captains for more details. But none of them had visited the island, or heard of anyone who had been there. This naturally made me still more curious and I began to hunt eagerly in all the available books. From the scanty information I found here and there I was able to construct the following picture of the island on which for several weeks we had set all our hopes.

Starbuck, so named after a British whaler captain who discovered the island in 1823, is about five miles long and almost two and a half miles wide at the widest point.

A fringing coral reef, about 1000 yards wide, against which the sea breaks violently, surrounds the island completely, and there is no sheltered anchorage or landing-place.

Like most atolls, Starbuck is very low, and no part of the island stands more than fifteen feet above sea level. When a cyclone, or a volcanic eruption on the sea bottom, causes a particularly heavy swell the waves often wash right over the island.

On the other hand, Starbuck differs from most of the South Sea atolls in that the only vegetation consists of clumps of grass and a few scattered bushes, none of which are more than three feet high or have any eatable fruit.

Apart from a narrow belt of sand along the shore, the greater part of the island is covered either with sea-birds' guano or a thick layer of salt from evaporated sea water, which has the unusual effect of making Starbuck, at a distance, resemble a great ice-floe. Of course there is no drinking water at all.

The first and only time that any human being attempted to settle on Starbuck was at the beginning of the 1870's, when some hyper-optimistic Americans, after several dangerous capsizings, landed with a couple of dozen native workers to collect guano. They were immediately surrounded by such dense clouds of screaming sea-birds that all conversation was impossible, but nevertheless took a walk round the island, in the course of which they found many bleached human bones and wreckage from at least seven different vessels. But even more unbearable than the ceaseless screaming of the birds were the heat and the blinding reflection of the sun's rays, and the Americans quickly gave up their hopeless attempt. Since then no one seems to have set foot on Starbuck, and few ships have passed near the inhospitable island.

Another discovery, almost equally unpleasant, which I made after our rescue was that Starbuck, at that moment, was included in the wide sea area round Christmas Island that was closed to all shipping on account of atomic bomb experiments.

But, as I have said, we were completely ignorant of all this at midday on August 16, 1958, and it was with great and genuine sorrow that I altered course and steered away.

Chapter 8

TOWARDS SAMOA

The mere fact that we had missed Starbuck was in itself very distressing. But as Eric and I saw it, even worse was that we were now so high up towards the Equator and so far west that our prospects of reaching Penrhyn had been gravely endangered. This upset us all the more because we knew well that Penrhyn—or Tongereva as it is called by Polynesians—was inhabited and was often visited by yachts on their way to or from Tahiti. Of course there was still a possibility that the north-easterly wind might gradually become a little more northerly and help us to reach the island. But unfortunately it was most probable that we should be obliged to go on to Samoa, in which case we must expect to spend at least another month on board *Tahiti Nui III*.

When I pointed out to my comrades, as tactfully as possible, that we had best prepare for a long voyage and proposed that we should ration our food and water still more strictly, Jean and Hans awoke from their apathy with surprising speed and began to protest vigorously. The gist of their vehement arguments was naturally that all further rationing was unnecessary, as we should soon be at Penrhyn. Had I not already said that we should be able to get ashore there? I replied angrily that we had missed our chance by not setting a course for Penrhyn at once and that they knew very well whose fault that was—an answer which scarcely contributed to the restoration of harmony on board.

As our lives depended on how we managed our small supplies, I resolved to have my way at all costs. So without wasting any more time in futile bickering, I opened our provisions box and made a list of the contents. This did not take long, for all we had left was approximately:

13 lb. fermented rice
11 lb. lentils
4½ lb. flour
2 packets of macaroni
2 tins of sausages
1 tin of cooked salmon
1 tin of corned beef
8 tins of mixed fruit
12 tins of condensed milk
4 pots of honey
7 small packets of raisins
2¼ lb. chocolate powder.

The few tins of preserves would last for only one or two meals, so the most sensible thing was certainly to treat them as a kind of iron ration, only to be touched in extremity. In my opinion we had only just as much honey, raisins and condensed milk as Eric needed. This meant that 13 lb. of rice, 11 lb. of lentils, 4½ lb. of flour and two packets of macaroni were all that remained for the rest of us. But none of these articles of food could be cooked without fire, and the only fire we could produce was with the help of the gas cooker. But we had only one bottle of gas left, and that was not nearly full, so it was completely out of the question to try to cook the hard lentils or make pancakes of flour. Having reluctantly eliminated this part of our supplies, I came to the depressing conclusion that we should have to live almost entirely on fermented rice and any fish we were able to catch.

As for drinking water, we had one brim-full ten-gallon tank. We should therefore be able to allow ourselves each three coffee cups of water a day and let Eric have a double ration.

As I had expected, my rationing programme aroused violent opposition. My comrades seemed to find it particularly hard to understand that the best way of saving gas and drinking water was to cook rice only every other day (but in sufficient quantities for two meals) and to cook it with sea water. Nor did they seem entirely convinced that Eric, who again had a high temperature, needed a double water ration and more nourishing food (i.e., honey, raisins and condensed milk) than the rest of us. After long discussions they finally agreed to my proposal, but showed plainly that they were dissatisfied with it.

Next day I raised the question of how we were to divide the steering watches, which was at least as important a question. I wanted to be free from steering watches during the day at all costs in order to be able to make observations, look after the lashings and repair any damage that might have been done, so I asked to be allowed to do all my watches consecutively during the first half of the night. No one protested this time, and thenceforward our watch roster was as follows:

18-00: Alain
00-02: Juanito
02-04: Hans
04-06: Jean
06-10: Juanito
10-14: Hans
14-18: Jean

Twenty-four long hours of watch-keeping passed. To my great joy and relief, *Tahiti Nui III* proved to be a notably fast sailer, for when I took the altitude of the sun on August 17th we were as much as fifty miles nearer Penrhyn. But, unfortunately, the wind had at the same time been getting more and more into the east and had driven us more than ten miles off our course, which meant that our prospects of reaching the island were already practically nil. Another rather bad omen was that the only fish we saw in the neighbourhood of the raft was our faithful brown shark, which evidently had not been deceived by our change of vessel. But instead of admitting that the strict rationing was really justified, Jean and Hans began to sulk and to be unpleasant to me. Juanito, who had behaved impeccably since we had abandoned *Tahiti Nui II,* seemed, on the contrary, to be resigned to his fate and gave me willing help with various minor jobs.

Next day, when I was in the middle of my calculations, it occurred to me that I could do them out better if I had something hard to put the paper on, and I therefore turned round in order to ask Juanito to saw off a suitable piece of masonite which projected from Eric's box. Juanito was at the helm, and I therefore asked Jean if he would do me this small service. Jean got up at once and took out the saw: but he had hardly taken hold of the piece of masonite when Juanito quite unexpectedly exclaimed in a menacing tone:

'Don't you dare to touch it!'

We all stared at him in astonishment. Was this the beginning of a new and serious crisis, or only a passing whim?

'But, my dear Juanito, what objection can you have to our sawing off a little bit of masonite?' asked Jean amiably, when he had recovered from his first surprise.

But the only answer was a still fiercer admonition:

'Don't you hear what I say? Don't touch the masonite!'

This was more than I could stand and from the disciplinary point of view was more than could be tolerated. I controlled my anger with the greatest possible effort, rose slowly, took the saw from Jean and, without saying a word, began to saw the masonite. Juanito, foaming with rage, dropped the steering oar, took a step forward and bellowed in my ear, shaking his fist:

'Don't you understand that the masonite is protecting my things?'

I did not give the smallest sign of understanding and went on sawing as if Juanito did not exist. Juanito repeated his threats and his curious 'explanation' several times; then he suddenly let his hands fall feebly to his sides and quite unexpectedly said in a whining voice:

'I want my share of the food, too.'

At last I understood the cause of Juanito's new crisis. It was clear that he had taken the rationing as badly as Jean and Hans, but had not dared to give expression to his dissatisfaction, and all his suppressed annoyance had at last exploded. Conscious that I was beginning to get the upper hand, I sat down as soon as I had sawn off the piece of masonite and tried to give the impression of being very busy. Juanito, deprived of his chief adversary in this disappointing manner, no longer knew what line to take, and after looking round uncertainly for a few moments, as if seeking help from Jean and Hans, he finally began steering again, to my inexpressible relief.

Although I had managed to keep my end up this time, I was none the less dispirited, for I felt that my victory was not durable. I became still more depressed when Jean and Hans, by more or less covert allusions, made me aware that in fact they shared Juanito's view that we ought to divide all the food and water equally between us. Later in the afternoon, when we had all calmed down, I tried once more to make them realize that it might be more than a month before we reached land, and that we were therefore compelled to ration our provisions very strictly. To give greater emphasis to my words I again gravely assured them that if everyone received his share at once the result could not fail to be disastrous, as those who finished their rations first would certainly not consent to die of starvation under the eyes of their more sensible and economical comrades.

But the best argument of all I kept for the last: that in any case it was impossible to share out most of our food supplies, for the simple reason that the contents of the preserve tins would not keep once they were opened and that we had not enough gas for each of us to cook his rations when and how he liked. This they were all obliged to admit. But they were quick to point out that several of our other articles of food could easily be divided up—for example, the twelve tins of condensed milk and the seven packets of raisins. The miserable discussion ended in their insisting that we should divide *equally* everything that could be divided. This showed clearly that the real cause of their shabby demand—as on the occasion a month earlier when we had first disputed rationing—was a desire to be avenged on Eric for all our misfortunes. For Eric was the only person on board who had any special rationing privileges, modest as these were.

Eric had a recipe, as simple as it was attractive, for maintaining discipline on board: he advised me quite audibly to give all rebellious members of the crew a good thrashing, and if that did no good, simply to chuck them overboard. My only objection to these disciplinary measures was that an attempt to apply them could just as well end in Eric and myself being chucked overboard instead. I therefore tried, when I was at last able to think the problem over in peace and quiet during my solitary evening watch, to find another and a better solution. I soon realized that I was quite helpless if my three comrades joined forces. The captain of a cargo ship had at least one excellent weapon at his disposal in the event of a threatened mutiny—he could read out the ship's articles and threaten the mutineers with severe punishment when the ship arrived at her destination. This would have no effect in our case, for no one on board was bound by any ship's articles, and our destination now seemed without much doubt to be the bottom of the sea.

So, after having turned and twisted the problem till my head ached, I was compelled to admit to myself that the only way of avoiding open mutiny was to share out the condensed milk and raisins as quickly as possible. To be quite honest, I regretted this new concession more on grounds of discipline than for Eric's sake, for anyway he ate so little now that his rations of milk and raisins, and my own, would certainly last till the end of the voyage, which, whatever form it took, could not be far off. Moreover, it would be a great relief to Eric, too, to avoid all further rationing trouble.

So next morning—August 19th—I told my comrades briefly that I was willing to meet their wishes, and gave each crew member two tins of condensed milk and a packet and a half of raisins. The remaining two tins of condensed milk I stowed away in Eric's box under their eyes. Fortunately, no objections at all were offered to this. But to my disappointment this concession did not much lighten the general mood of depression and when, a little later, I slid down into the water to tighten some lashings which were becoming loose, Jean, Hans and Juanito looked on as apathetically as on every previous occasion when I had done any repairs, and did not once offer a helping hand.

The member of the crew who caused me most anxiety at this time was Jean, hitherto always so reliable and helpful: he was now either completely indifferent to his fate or idiotically confident that we should soon reach Penrhyn. Most unluckily, by some curious chance, he was particularly apathetic and slack every time he was at the helm, with the unpleasant result that we drifted sideways and got drenched quite unnecessarily. After patiently enduring Jean's capricious behaviour for a whole twenty-four hours I finally lost my temper and gave him a good telling-off during his morning watch on August 20th. The result was most unexpected. Jean listened quietly to my outburst, and contented himself with the ironical remark:

'It must be that honey in the box on the port side which is pulling the steering oar the wrong way.'

I was so furious that I was within an ace of flying at him, but fortunately checked myself at the last moment. Wild, confused thoughts chased each other through my brain, but I soon realized that I was chiefly to blame. A long time ago I had been stupid enough to adopt the dangerous policy of making concessions, and the only thing I could do now was to continue this policy to the end. But often as I told myself that I ought to share out the honey, too, to avoid all similar scenes, I could not bring myself to do it until next day. When I opened the provision box to give a pot of honey each to Jean, Hans and Juanito, I caught sight of the bag of chocolate powder and hastened to divide this equally between us. Having done so, I shut the box again with a loud bang.

This disagreeable episode took place on the morning of August 21st. Only a few hours later we passed the longitude of Penrhyn as much as 40 miles north of the island. Jean, who till this moment had clung firmly to his irrational conviction that we should somehow or other reach the island, collapsed altogether, and again and again I heard him muttering something about our being like wandering Jews who had no home. I would rather that he had screamed, wept and cursed, but he continued to suffer in silence, which in the long run was as unbearable for the rest of us as for himself. To make him forget his despair—and at the same time to obtain a necessary addition to our food supply—I tried to persuade him to try his luck as a fisherman again, and after many long sighs he actually took out his spear-gun and slipped into the water.

My most daring hopes were realized almost at once, for a big dolphin—the first we had seen for a long time—came gliding gently through the water and offered itself as a target. Although Jean was by no means in his old form, he pulled himself together and was able to spear it at the second attempt, but when he tried to haul in his catch he fumbled and was so slow about it that a small shark, about three feet long, snapped the fish up. Jean reloaded quickly and with unexpected energy sent the arrow deep into the shark's side. It was a most thoughtless action, for Jean had only one arrow left, and there were nine chances in ten that the shark would break the slender line and disappear with the arrow. While the rest of us watched with our hearts in our mouths, Jean tugged and jerked furiously at the line. Both arrow and line held, and at last the shark lay kicking on the deck. I felt almost relieved when I saw that it was not our faithful companion of several months past. Shark's flesh is no great delicacy, but we were no longer very particular about our food and cut up Jean's catch with satisfaction. The pieces which we could not devour at once we carefully dried in the sun in the hope that we might thus be able to keep them for future needs.

The capture of the shark and the business of drying it gave us something to think about, but soon our spirits were as low as ever. A new oppressive factor was the great heat, which dried up all the pores in our bodies and compelled us to dilute our small water rations with greater and greater quantities of sea water.

Now more than ever it seemed that our only chance of saving our lives was to reach Samoa as quickly as possible. It was therefore with helpless fury that during the next few days we saw the wind slowly shift from east to south-east, which gave us an almost due westerly course, no matter how forcibly we put the helm over to starboard. I looked at the chart oftener and oftener, and with increasing anxiety. Our position was a miserable nine degrees south. The Samoan Islands lay spread in a wide arc between the thirteenth and sixteenth degrees of latitude. So if the south-easterly wind continued it was far from certain that we could steer down to them in time. The more unfavourable our course became, the stronger became Jean and Hans's suspicions that I was not a competent navigator, and on top of all other worries I was now compelled to explain to them daily and hourly why our real positions did not agree with those which they themselves had reached by God knew what methods.

Exactly a week after the first general stock-taking I went through our supplies again and made the not altogether unexpected discovery that we had already finished more than a third of our rice and nearly half our water. Our prospects of reaching land or being rescued by a ship before we died of hunger or thirst suddenly seemed to be infinitesimally small, and I was overcome by mental and physical weariness. What was the use of prolonging our sufferings? Just at that moment, when I felt gloomier than ever, I heard Eric muttering something and I moved a little nearer his box. He had aged a great deal of late and his temperature was always high. He often talked at random during his long, trance-like periods of sleep. Evidently unaware that I heard him, he repeated several times in succession the same despairing prayer:

'Good God, I don't care how it ends, if only the end comes quickly.'

I was on the verge of tears and remained seated and half-dazed by Eric's box. But in some strange manner my desire to live soon welled up again. Perhaps there was no more remarkable explanation for the change in me than the fact that, unlike Eric, I was young and healthy. I pulled myself together and forced myself to reflect coolly and soberly on the problems of our food supply. I had often wondered whether there was not some other way of preparing lentils than cooking them on the gas cooker. But only now did I at last realize that what was wanted was a practical test instead of more head-scratchings. To save my comrades unnecessary disappointment and myself unnecessary disputes I waited till my solitary night watch to make a little experiment. All I did was to put a handful of lentils to soak in a cup of sea water. When I tasted them in secret next morning, they were naturally pretty salty, but soft enough to chew. I was encouraged by this success, but was unwilling to tell my raft-mates anything about my experiment for fear that they would immediately demand that the lentils be shared out.

At last I dared to propose that we should reduce our water ration to two cups each daily. Juanito immediately announced that he would take no more watches if I tried to play him such a shabby trick. This made me fear another stormy scene. But when I saw that Jean and Hans were still too broken to make any serious protest I plucked up courage and told Juanito firmly that in that case I would take his watches as well as my own. He did not reply, and immediately afterwards, when it was his turn, he relieved Jean without objection.

That same night, while I was on watch, it began to rain. I shouted jubilantly to my comrades to come and help me spread a sail to catch it. I had expected that this wonderful news would restore their courage. But only Hans and Juanito at last sat up, and neither of them seemed particularly cheered at this much needed addition to our drinking water. I handed over the steering to Juanito and hastened to cover up our last usable wireless receiver, on which our lives now hung, as it was impossible to make any exact observations without the wireless time signals. At the same time, I took the trouble to bend over Jean to wake him. To my surprise he was already wide awake, but instead of getting up he declared wearily that to collect rain water would only prolong our sufferings unnecessarily, and that he at any rate preferred a speedy death. When I continued my efforts to persuade him he turned his back. We managed very well without his help, and in less than half an hour filled both our ten-gallon tanks and our last three-gallon demijohn, but my pleasure was considerably damped by the new problem created by Jean's nervous breakdown.

But I soon forgot this problem for another and much more important one. The first welcome shower was quickly followed by a new and much less welcome downpour, which in turn proved to be only the prelude to a violent thunderstorm. A few hours later a regular gale was blowing, and our poor outrigger raft, flung by the waves this way and that like a withered autumn leaf, was creaking in her joints oftener and oftener and more and more ominously. With the raft lying so deep there was also a danger that Eric's box, with the wireless and our navigation instruments, would be swept away. I hesitated for a very long time before trying to strengthen the lashings, but when one of the floats suddenly came loose I abandoned all timorous inhibitions and jumped in.

Not even at this critical moment did I get any help from my comrades: Jean and Hans looked on indifferently as usual, while Juanito, incredible as it may sound, was fast asleep. As time passed, and I became even colder and wetter, my dislike of this work on the lashings, which had to be done over and over again, gradually disappeared, and at last it was a sheer relief to crawl down into the warm sea and escape for a little while from the torturing wind.

The gale and pouring rain lasted for nearly forty-eight hours, and when at last the weather improved a little in the early morning hours of August 26th, we were all more dead than alive. I felt that a good hot meal would do wonders, and proposed that we should open some of the tins of preserves that constituted our iron rations. My comrades nodded approval with extraordinarily indifferent faces, but when we had gorged ourselves on a big dish of macaroni, garnished with the contents of our two last tins of sausage, and each of us had gulped down his large helping of preserved fruit, their spirits really rose a little. Even Eric, who ate only a few mouthfuls of condensed milk and honey, seemed to be slowly reviving. At any rate, he did not seem any worse than before the storm, which no doubt was mainly because we had carefully covered him up with windproof clothes and a protecting sheet of canvas. Early in the afternoon the sun peeped out again, and when the wind returned after a long interval of dead calm it was no longer south-easterly but north-easterly. Next day our position was as much as 30 miles farther south, and the wind was still just as favourable.

Two of the northern Cook Islands, Manihiki and Rakahanga, now lay right in our course, only about 120 miles away. As soon as Jean and Hans discovered this, they brightened up and began to talk of our being saved in the near future with the same naïve confidence of which they had already given proof twice before, when we were approaching Starbuck and Penrhyn. I shuddered to think how they would react if we missed these islands, too, which we probably would, experience having shown that the wind could not be relied upon. Eric was too tired and ill to be able to give me any advice this time, so I began a kind of dialogue with myself to find out if there really was any way to improve the steering so that we could make a landing on one of these islands even if the wind changed slightly. Having rejected half a dozen impracticable plans one by one, I had at last another, and in my opinion much better, idea, which I hastened to put before my raft-mates:

'Look here, boys, how about building a *Tahiti Nui IV?*'

This brief introduction had the intended effect, for my three comrades moved nearer to me at once, and their astonished faces showed plainly that I had succeeded in arousing their interest. I therefore continued my little address without delay, more or less as follows:

'What we need now more than anything is greater mobility and range. We are in the same hole now as a fortnight ago, when *Tahiti Nui II* was nothing but a wreck which looked like drifting past Starbuck. That time we got out of the hole by building this outrigger raft. So why not do the same thing again and build a still smaller raft, so light that we could paddle her the last bit of the voyage towards the islands, if we see that we're drifting past?'

'We four can certainly stand the hardships, but how will Eric manage, who can't even endure getting wet?' Hans objected.

'We can't even take this raft to bits without all tumbling into the water,' said Jean critically.

I had expected these objections and had my answer ready at once:

'What I have in mind is a very primitive paddle raft made of two spars kept together by a few planks, which can serve as seats at the same time. As we're lucky enough to have a couple of extra spars on board, there's no need for us to take *Tahiti Nui III* to pieces. Of course we can't send Eric ashore on a couple of spars, but that doesn't matter, for three of us must stay here on board *Tahiti Nui III* while two of us—I don't think *Tahiti Nui IV* will take more—paddle ashore to get help. If those who stay on board get in the sail at the moment when the shore party start, *Tahiti Nui III* will certainly drift past the island so slowly that the natives will be able to come out with a few big canoes and take them off. If the natives can't come out, or haven't big enough canoes, our shore party will save themselves by remaining on the island. As for those who drift on, their provisions will last longer with only two men on board, so they'll gain something too.'

'It sounds all right,' said Juanito. 'But what'll happen if the island's uninhabited?'

'Then the shore party will have to choose quickly between staying on the island and trying to paddle after *Tahiti Nui III*.'

Although my plan of escape involved many risks, my comrades at once agreed to try it. It was especially pleasant to see Jean liven up and become himself again. After a long and amicable discussion we agreed that I should stay on board *Tahiti Nui III*, together with Eric, as I was the only one of us who understood navigation, and that the shore party should consist of Jean and Juanito. By a lucky chance we had taken with us the two paddles which Juanito had once made long ago, when he had wanted to go off alone on his three-cornered raft, and they proved to be of exactly the right length. After we had worked a few nails loose we had no difficulty in fastening the two extra spars together. The preparations had not taken more than an hour in all.

The north-easterly wind continued on August 28th and a good way into August 29th. But at midday on August 29th, immediately after we had learnt with satisfaction that we were thirty miles due east of Rakahanga, it began to shift to easterly again. According to Eric only

Manihiki was inhabited. But with the wind we now had it was extremely uncertain whether we would be able to run down to this island, while our chances of making Rakahanga seemed very good. So we unhesitatingly set course for Rakahanga, although we were a little farther from it than from the more southerly island. I hung over the compass almost all night and began to make observations as soon as the sun rose on August 30th. These showed that we were still approaching the island, but so slowly that I soon began to fear that we should not get there before nightfall. At 4 P.M. according to my calculations, we had still ten miles to go. So there was no longer any hope of running the raft ashore there in daylight, which made our situation very awkward. We had to choose between three possibilities:

(1) We could try to cruise to and fro off Rakahanga till the sun rose.

(2) We could try to go on to Manihiki.

(3) We could steer straight for Rakahanga and try to land there in the dark.

During the afternoon we had seen to our alarm that we were in the middle of a strong southward current, and that the wind seemed to be veering again. So that if we chose alternatives (1) or (2) we ran a risk of being swept right through the gap between the islands, and this idea we found so intolerable that we resolved almost without discussion to go right in towards Rakahanga. We also decided unanimously to open our last tins of preserves at once and so strengthen ourselves for the hardships to come. As soon as we had filled our stomachs we emptied the water tanks and stowed our few personal belongings in them. Then we threw all heavy, bulky objects overboard.

While we were making these preparations I heard Eric, who had insisted on our helping him to sit up so that he should be able to keep a look out, muttering something about the navigation, as though dissatisfied. At last I became a little uneasy myself and did the calculation for my last observation over again. It was correct. We had really been ten miles east of Rakahanga at 4 P.M., so we ought to see the island soon.

The great moment came at exactly 5:15 P.M., and it was Eric who first saw the dark line of palms on the horizon, showing that I had navigated correctly. I contented myself with pressing Eric's hand in silence, and Juanito also took the great discovery very calmly, while Jean and Hans yelled and laughed like madmen. It grew dark immediately after six, and we suddenly felt ourselves cruelly consigned to oblivion and annihilation. But this time Providence was unusually kind to us, for at about eight a round, full moon rose swiftly out of the sea and restored our sight. As far as I could judge, we were now one sea mile at most from the island, and below the dark line of the coconut palms a white line of foaming breakers could now be clearly seen. I passed the steering oar to Juanito and took up a position in the bows to get a closer sight of the breakers. I knew from my time as a seaman in copra schooners in French Polynesia that there are often gaps here and there in the reef which surrounds a coral island. If only I could find such a gap we should have a better chance of escaping alive from the dangerous adventure which a stranding on the weather side of a coral island must always be.

When we came so near that we could hear the loud roaring of the breakers, for want of a better drogue we pushed the two spars, which a few days before we had audaciously christened *Tahiti Nui IV*, into the water and tied them astern of the raft with a rope. This, as we intended, put a further slight brake on our speed, and also prevented the raft from turning round.

About the same time Eric, to my alarm, expressed a wish to sit on the top of his box. This seemed to me to be quite the most dangerous place on board, as the box was fastened to the crossbeams with only a few nails. And so, instead, he sat aft between Jean and Hans. With Juanito still at the steering oar and myself as look-out in the bows, we slowly approached the high breakers. To my disappointment I was unable to detect any gaps in the reef, but I consoled myself with the reflection that at any rate it seemed to be high tide. There was therefore a good chance that the raft would slide up on to the reef without being crushed, which is the usual consequence of running on to a reef at low water.

When we were only a few yards away I hastily sprang across to the stern. Eric was still sitting between Jean and Hans and had put his arms round their necks for safety. The thundering of the surf was now so loud that we could no longer make ourselves heard, but Eric smiled at me with an expression of relief and triumph on his emaciated face which was more eloquent than many words. I glanced at my watch. It was a few minutes to nine. Immediately afterwards I felt the stern lifted up and the raft tipped over forward. After that I do not know just what happened, but I came up to the surface again with an aching head, and my poor lungs were at last able to inhale a little air.

The first of my comrades whom I saw was Juanito, who was standing up to his waist in the water on a coral block a little nearer the shore. Then the heads of Jean and Hans appeared, dangerously close to a drum which was bobbing about. Only Eric was missing. It occurred to me that he might have been caught under the upset raft. I dived down and groped along the logs, feeling hopeful and frightened at the same time; but as I came again to the surface I saw Eric's skinny form close beside the raft. I was with him in a few seconds and caught him under the arms. It was terribly hard to keep his face above water because of the waves, but Jean quickly came to my help: we both got astride a row of floats and at last succeeded in hauling Eric up out of the water. It was only when we began to take off some of his heavy, waterlogged clothes that it occurred to me how foolish we had been not to undress him before we reached the breakers. Even a strong man and a swimmer would certainly have gone to the bottom at once if he wore so many clothes, and poor Eric was weak and ill and a non-swimmer into the bargain. Time after time the words 'too late' rang in my head.

We examined Eric as well as we could. He was quite unconscious but had no visible injury. We therefore were sure that we could save him if we could only get him ashore quickly and apply artificial respiration. It was not far to the beach: a hundred yards at most. But the raft was held back by the backwash from the breakers. Hans and Juanito tried to drag her nearer to the beach, but the end of that was that they got underneath her and were in danger of having their heads crushed. To swim to the beach with Eric, through the treacherous eddies which barred the way, was a dangerous undertaking which we dared not attempt in our exhausted state. Jean and I, therefore, remained sitting helplessly on the raft with Eric between us till at last an unusually big wave drew her in towards the beach. Halfway, however, she ran on to a block of coral and stuck fast. When Jean slid cautiously down into the water he found that he touched bottom without difficulty, so we hastened to wade ashore with Eric. I happened to catch sight of the illuminated hands of my wrist-watch, and hardly believed my eyes when I saw that it was a quarter to twelve: almost three hours had passed since the raft had capsized.

Hans came to meet and help us some time before we reached the shore. He had fallen down into a hole in the coral reef and his face was badly cut. Nevertheless he was not half as anxious on his own account as on Juanito's. He told us that Juanito had scrambled up on the beach more than an hour before and had disappeared at once. We told Hans to go and look for Juanito and hurriedly prepared a bed of dry palm leaves, on which we laid Eric.

We had no matches, so that we could not see if he was breathing, but when I laid my ear against his breast I thought I heard a faint sound. This gave us hope and we started artificial respiration without delay. Time passed, and we relieved one another more frequently as we panted from our exertions. Our greatest worry in the increasing night cold and wind was how to keep Eric warm, and when Jean got the idea that waves might have thrown up a sail, in which we could wrap him, I told him to make a short reconnaissance along the shore. But he soon came back and in a melancholy voice told me that the raft had disappeared. The only useful object he had found was a little bottle of pure alcohol, which had evidently fallen out of the medicine chest. We eagerly moistened Eric's tongue and gums, and then obstinately continued our attempts to revive him. Not until Eric's limbs began to stiffen did we grasp at last the reason why he had been cold for so long.

Worn out and dumb with despair, we sank down on the ground beside our dead captain. It was four o'clock. Neither Juanito nor Hans had returned. There was no sign that the island was inhabited.

Chapter 9

RAKAHANGA

Suddenly a slight noise made us start. We listened intently and could clearly hear the scrunching sound of crushed coral stones. Someone seemed to be making his way through the scrub. I had not yet decided whether to call to the invisible walker or not when the silhouette of a short, familiar figure appeared against the pale sky quite close to us. Much relieved, I said:

'Where have you been, Juanito?'

'I've been looking for help. But what has happened? Is Eric—?'

'Yes, he's dead.'

Juanito bowed his head, and next moment I heard him break into agonized sobs. His genuine despair suddenly made me feel tenderly towards him, and I forgave him for all the wrong he had done to Eric and me.

'Calm down now and tell me what you've been up to,'

I said kindly a little later, when he seemed unable to pull himself together.

'I saw a light,' he said in a tearful voice. 'Somewhere to the south. Not very far off. I'd nearly got to it when I turned back.'

'But why did you turn back? Wasn't it your idea to get help?'

'Yes, but I wanted to let you know as soon as possible that I had seen a light.'

Warned by my depressing experiences in the past, I made no attempt to understand Juanito's proceedings and simply asked if he had seen anything of Hans. He shook his head vigorously.

While waiting for Hans to turn up I walked down to the beach to see if by any chance any more things had been washed up from the wreck, but to my disappointment I only found a few tins of Nescafé. A cup of good hot coffee was just what we needed, but unfortunately we had neither matches nor drinking water. So the sight of the tins only annoyed me and I kicked them away as far I could. I waded aimlessly out into the surf and without any definite plan. The only reward for my trouble was that I immediately detected a triangular shark's fin moving uneasily to and fro just at the place where the raft had capsized. Could it really be the brown shark which had followed us so faithfully for several months? If so, it was not surprising if it was now both bewildered and disappointed. I returned to our primitive camping place empty-handed and disgruntled.

I did not need to worry for long as to what might have

happened to Hans, for only a quarter of an hour later there was a crackling in the scrub again, and he staggered towards us and sank down on the ground weary to the point of collapse. He had gone northward and he too had seen a light. Convinced by Juanito's and Hans's independent evidence that the island was inhabited, I resolved to get help as quickly as possible. As Hans was too exhausted for another long walk, I asked him to stay and watch over our dead captain, and told Juanito to show Jean and me the way to the light which he had seen.

The sky had already begun to lighten, and we could now clearly distinguish through the palm trunks a shining lagoon on the other side of the strip of land on which we now were. After a search we found a narrow path which followed the edge of the lagoon southwards, and set out along it. Here and there along the path lay great heaps of coconuts recently cut in half, but nowhere did we see the human beings who must have carried out this work. After half an hour's quick walking we came to a wide natural channel which joined the sea and the lagoon, and as Juanito eagerly assured us that he had crossed the channel on his night walk we jumped in. We could only just get a foothold, and the current was so strong that we were nearly washed out into the sea several times. When we had swum and waded over four or five more of these wide channels in quick succession, Juanito was no longer sure that we were going the right way. But we had no desire to turn back, especially as we now saw with our own eyes that the island was absolutely round. We therefore went on, in the certainty that we must come upon the inhabitants sooner or later, even if Juanito might have got the points of the compass a bit confused.

It was a few minutes past seven, so that we had been going for nearly two hours, when we came out into a glade close to the shore of the lagoon and saw a village consisting of two rows of houses on both sides of a straight street. Most of the houses were made of plaited palm leaves and bamboos, but there were also a few built of planks and stones with ugly rusty roofs of corrugated iron. Every house was surrounded by a garden with coconut palms, bread-fruit trees and brilliant flower-beds. There was no one at all in the impeccably clean main street, which was covered with coral sand, and this surprised me a good deal until I remembered that it was Sunday.

The first person we came upon was a well-built middle-aged Polynesian in a red loin-cloth who was strolling about in the garden in front of a yellow bamboo hut. When he caught sight of us he turned pale with terror—no doubt he thought we were ghosts, an understandable mistake, as we looked so awful—and turned to flee.

'*A tiai rii* (wait a minute),' I tried on him in Tahitian.

He stopped short, and his features showed clearly that fear was giving place to intense curiosity.

'*Ua ite oe i te parau Tahiti?* (Can you speak Tahitian?)' I continued without much hope of getting an answer in the affirmative.

A broad smile cleft the man's face and he answered quickly in excellent Tahitian.

'You've come to the right man. I'm the only person on the island who speaks Tahitian. I learnt the language in my young days, when I was a seaman in a Tahitian schooner.'

I hastened to tell him, in the fewest possible words, what had happened. The news was too remarkable for the man to be able to keep to himself a second longer than necessary, and he rushed out into the village street yelling like a newspaper boy trying to get rid of the last extra edition. The villagers came running at once from every direction, as if they had just been sitting and waiting for something of the kind to happen, and we were soon surrounded by at least a hundred chattering men, women and children. Their language closely resembled the Polynesian dialect which is spoken in the Tuamotu Islands, so that I understood them very well. Also, some of them could speak a little English. I explained to them again and again, in Tahitian and English, that one of our comrades had been left in the palm grove and asked them to show us the way to the chief's house, but they were all too busy discussing our persons to accede to our wish.

At last my Tahitian-speaking friend seemed to take pity on me, and gave me his hand. But instead of going to see the chief he took me straight to his own house, of which I was not aware until he had forced me down into a chair and placed before me a large dish of grilled flying fish and bread-fruit. I tried to protest, but he immediately brushed aside all my objections with a curt:

'Be quiet and eat!'

The temptation was too great, and to the evident delight of my host I attacked the flying fish (which smelt delicious) and the bread-fruit with a voracious appetite. If I had been on a French island I should certainly have been given a bottle of red wine with which to wash down my food, but Rakahanga was under British (or to be more correct, New Zealand) sovereignty, so of course I got a large cup of tea instead. Just as I was swallowing the last morsel of bread-fruit a messenger arrived and curtly ordered me to accompany him. The messenger made for a large cement house farther down the street, and there I found Jean and Juanito. They had been looked after by other families and were as full of food as I was.

A few seconds later a powerfully built man came out of the cement house, and I realized at once from his dignified bearing and majestic appearance that he was the island chief. His name was Turuta, and he spoke excellent English. Without wasting any time on long preliminary phrases, such as Polynesian etiquette really demanded, I told him impatiently what had happened. Turuta replied, quite unruffled:

'I have sent two canoes already to fetch your comrade and your dead captain. But we must not forget you. Please come in.'

I had thought that the cement house was Chief Turuta's office or official residence, but when I obeyed him, to my surprise I entered a little hospital. My first instinct was to say right out that we were not so done up that we needed to be taken to hospital, but then I remembered all our cuts and scratches and sat down obediently on the wooden bench to which Turuta ushered us.

The treatment began curiously enough with the male nurse, who was Turuta's brother, producing a bottle and pouring out a small glass of the contents for each of us. We sniffed cautiously at the clear, mahogany-coloured liquid. It was brandy! We emptied our glasses at a draught and held them out to be refilled. The male nurse, however, declared gravely that it was the only bottle of spirits in the island and put it back into the medicine chest. We regretted at once that we had not tried to look rather more ill. The next stage of the treatment was almost as pleasant, for it consisted of a shower-bath of cool rainwater from one of the large cisterns next to the hospital. Finally the male nurse put plenty of iodine and sticking-plaster on our badly damaged arms and legs.

Just as we were leaving the hospital, wearing clean clothes borrowed for us in the village by the male nurse, the men whom the chief has sent out to the scene of the disaster returned, carrying Eric's dead body between them on a modern stretcher. He still wore the same triumphant smile which I had seen just before we were drawn into the surf—clearly showing that the only thing that mattered for him at the time of his death, as during all his life, was to realize his dreams. Poor Hans, hollow-eyed and exhausted, came tottering along far behind. When he had been given the same treatment as the rest of us, he recovered sufficiently to limp across to a neighbouring house, where some kind villagers had prepared a good meal.

Chief Turuta's men told us that they had also found the shattered outrigger raft. They assured us that it was only the wooden frame which had been smashed, and they wondered very much where we had got the fine aluminium tanks. We suddenly felt impelled to write at once to the Belgian chemist in Lima who had almost forced them on us and thank him for having saved our lives. But unfortunately none of us could remember his name, so I hope that he will some day read this book and realize what an invaluable service he had rendered us.

While we were talking to Hans and the stretcher-bearers the chief has disappeared, but before long he came back and announced that by a lucky chance the administrator of the northern Cook Islands was just about to make his annual tour of inspection and would probably arrive at Rakahanga the very next day. When I asked how he knew this, Turuta replied with pride that there there was, of course, a wireless station on the island and that another of his brothers was its superintendent. With Turuta's kind permission we trudged over to the wireless station at once and sent a telegram to our expedition secretary Carlos Garcia-Palacios in Tahiti, who by that time must certainly have been rather anxious about us.

When we returned to the hospital Turuta's nursing brother had already dressed Eric in trousers, sandals, a white shirt and a striped tie. If I had not already seen many funeral wakes elsewhere in Polynesia I should certainly have made some objection to this rig-out, but knowing as I did that it was the natives' usual way of clothing their dead for burial, I said nothing. But one unusual detail struck me almost at once. Eric had also a white bandage round his head on a level with his forehead. When Turuta saw my astonished face, he handed me without a word a neat death certificate which he had just filled up. I read, in a regular and pretty hand, the words 'cause of death: Injuries to the back of the head and a broken neck'. There could no longer be any doubt. Eric had died from a blow on the back of the head when the raft turned round and not from drowning. So the many heavy clothes he had been wearing when we stranded had been of no significance whatever. I laid the death certificate down with a slight sense of relief. Turuta waited tactfully for some time before he spoke again. Then he said:

'Your captain died yesterday evening. According to our laws here in Cook Islands all deceased persons must be buried within twenty-four hours. I propose, therefore, that we bury your captain at three o'clock.'

The same law, dictated by reasons of health, exists in French Polynesia. I was therefore not in the least surprised at such haste and nodded approval.

'Good,' said Turuta. 'Now come with me and have a bit of food. It must be something awful to go hungry as you've been doing.'

We replied that it was not so long since we had eaten a good breakfast and that we had never been in serious danger of dying of starvation. But Turuta regarded these remarks as mere polite excuses, and without replying led us off to the village hall, a pretty house in the Polynesian style which was open on three sides. On the fourth side was a wall on which hung a long row of portraits of British kings and queens. The islanders' loyalty had fortunately not extended to the cooking of an English meal, for the dishes, which were all set out on an oblong table, in the middle of the hall, consisted exclusively of such Polynesian delicacies as chicken baked in an earth oven, roast bread-fruit, a salad of coconut sprouts and green drinking nuts.

Places were laid and chairs drawn up for only four, but practically the whole population of the island had assembled to wait on us. What we particularly appreciated was that two women immediately posted themselves behind each chair to chase away any flies which dared to disturb our meal. As at all Polynesian banquets, we were naturally also entertained by a party of men and women with good voices. To my surprise they had several Tahitian songs on their programme, but this, as I ought to have understood at once, was simply because they often listened to Radio Papeete. One of these songs was *Tahiti Nui*, a melancholy Tahitian song in praise of the island and having nothing but the name in common with our expedition. Evidently thinking, quite understandably, that we particularly liked this song, the natives sang it over and over again. The continually repeated refrain about Tahiti Nui, however, made me think of nothing but our disastrous raft expedition and depressed me. I therefore asked our private choir to sing a song about Rakahanga instead, and heard a rattling lively tune.

The only way in which we could show our keen appreciation of the islanders' kindness was, of course, to do honour to the dishes laid before us, so we methodically disposed of one course after another. Our heroic efforts were fortunately made a good deal easier by the unusual deliciousness of all the dishes, which stimulated our appetite and made it possible for us to put away far greater quantities of food than we had thought possible. So when the struggle was over and we looked round us in victorious pride, the dishes were almost empty. Unluckily Turuta came to the rather hasty conclusion that we had not yet had enough, and scarcely had we, with great difficulty, managed to rise from the table when he kindly invited us to accompany him home and take a light meal. We tried to explain to him that we needed a few hours' rest rather than more food, but for all our resistance we were compelled to swallow quite a lot more food before at last he let us sink down on to a few cool pandanus mats on his verandah.

Only after prolonged efforts was Turuta able to recall us to consciousness just before three o'clock. On the way to the church he proudly pointed out the school-house, a pretty building of coral stone. I asked in all innocence who did the teaching, and Turuta replied, with a certain surprise at my having asked such a stupid question, that of course he was also the island's schoolmaster. I was almost sure that in the next breath he would inform me that he was the island's clergyman as well, but when we arrived at the church it appeared that for some reason he had let one of his many brothers occupy this post.

Our dead captain now lay in a simple but tasteful coffin and was shrouded in a gaily-coloured cloth. When I looked more closely I saw that it was the Chilean flag which a sewing party at Constitucion had given us before our departure. Presumably, some of the islanders had found it on the shore near the scene of the disaster and given it to the clergyman, whose knowledge of foreign countries' flags was evidently a trifle hazy. In any case, there was no Tricolor on the island, and it would only have been painful to all parties to try to correct the mistake, so we pretended not to notice it. For that matter it was really not so unsuitable that the Chilean flag should accompany Eric to the grave, for he had loved Chile as a second fatherland and it was only thanks to Chilean help that we had been able to build our second raft.

Another thing which also worried me a little for a few moments was that Eric had formally belonged to the Catholic church. But he had never been a believing Catholic, and the only religion in which he had ever taken any interest was the old heathen Polynesian one. So all things considered it did not to my mind matter in the least that a Protestant clergyman was reading the funeral service.

After several long prayers and two movingly beautiful hymns four men lifted the coffin, and on a sign from the priest we all rose and followed them out of the church. The distance from the church to the cemetery was only a few hundred yards, but before we were halfway I was overcome by weariness and began to have unpleasant feelings of nausea. I saw as in a mist first Juanito and then Jean faint and be carried away. What happened to Hans I had no idea. Only with the greatest difficulty I succeeded in keeping on my legs till the grave had been filled, after which Turuta took me home and laid me down on the sleeping mat on the verandah, where I at once fell into a deep sleep.

When Turuta woke me again I felt so rested and well that I first suspected that I had slept for several days on end. But it was only Monday, and the sole reason why Turuta had not let me sleep longer was that the administrator of the northern Cook Islands had just arrived. He was accompanied by a judge, and when the two of them had listened to our story the judge declared that in accordance with the law he would hold an inquiry into the loss of the raft as soon as he had dealt with the few cases on hand. These were concerned mostly with stray pigs which had rooted up gardens and too-hilarious young men who had made disturbances at night. Nor did the administrator's task seem particularly exacting, for both Turuta and his brother had discharged their functions faultlessly. As we had nothing else to do we devoted the rest of the day to two occupations which still held the charm of novelty: we ate and slept.

The inquiry into the wreck made it necessary for us to go through the painful drama of the last few days in detail, and we were still depressed when we left the village hall, where all legal proceedings took place. But we soon had something else to think about. A telegram had come from Tahiti saying that a gunboat had been sent out to fetch us and might be expected to arrive at Rakahanga on Thursday afternoon. We began to search for objects from the wreck with renewed energy, and pack up the few things we had found already. Jean even went so far as to begin diving into the surf with a few athletic fellows, at the place where the raft had capsized. But the result was meagre in the extreme, for the only thing he succeeded in fishing up was our ruined radio apparatus. The various patrols which combed the shore from one end of the island to the other had much better luck, and when at last all the finds were neatly laid out in the village hall I found among them, to my boundless joy, not only our Polynesian wooden god but also, severely damaged, the galvanized iron jar in which, just before the shipwreck, I had stowed the log, the charts, my personal diary and my eight rolls of film. I trembled with eagerness as I emptied out the contents. Both the papers and the rolls of film were quite undamaged.

The French gunboat *Lotus* arrived early in the afternoon of September 4th, and as there was no gap in the reef through which she could enter the lagoon she laid to just outside the reef on the lee side of the island. The chief Turuta promptly manned several canoes and told the administrator and myself to take seats in the canoe which was under his own command.

The first person I ran up against on board *Lotus* was our devoted secretary, Carlos Garcia-Palacios, who embraced me with tears in his eyes. The next to embrace me was my comrade from the outward voyage in *Tahiti Nui I*, Francis Cowan. Behind him several French officers in well-preserved uniforms were waiting. Jean, Hans and Juanito followed closely in another canoe, and soon questions and answers were flying to and fro. In the deafening noise which arose our conversation soon became confused and inaudible in quality. But it did not matter. The main thing was that we could somehow give expression to our long pent-up feelings.

Turuta, as we expected, showed himself fully equal to the situation, for as soon as his new guests had landed he took them straight to the village hall, where the whole population was formed up in a square and greeted us with *God Save the Queen*. Of course this was followed by a tremendous dinner, and we astonished both ourselves and our friends by the huge quantities of food we put away. But practice, as everyone knows, makes perfect.

The captain of *Lotus* had orders to take Eric's body to Tahiti, so as soon as the dinner was over we went along to the pretty little cemetery and cautiously opened the fresh grave. We had hardly finished this melancholy task when it was time to dress for the great ball which the people of Rakahanga had resolved to hold in our honour. To many people such a mingling of sorrow and joy may seem lacking in taste, and we too had at first resisted the islanders' proposal. Chief Turuta and his subordinates had naturally misunderstood our unwillingness, for as they—and all Polynesians—see things, the dead, whose whole existence is one long feast, cannot possibly object to those who are left behind trying to find a little pleasure and diversion. At last we let them have their way, for we were convinced that it would be only humbug to try to make them respect a convention which to them was meaningless, and Eric hated nothing so much as humbug. But to tell the truth, I could not take part in the ball with the same enthusiasm as my Polynesian friends, and if—as often happens in those latitudes—the women had not repeatedly asked me to dance, I do not think I should have gone on to the floor at all.

I had not danced since February 14th, i.e., the evening before we left Constitucion, and I was still sore and stiff after the unusual exercise when I dragged myself up from my sleeping mat long after sunrise next morning. One of the main attractions of the ball had of course been a magnificent supper, whose aftereffects I still felt in my abdominal region. So I showed only very moderate enthusiasm when Chief Turuta came trotting up and announced that a last farewell meal had been laid for us and our friends from *Lotus* in the village hall, and I limped off slowly by a roundabout route so that I might become more or less myself again.

The good people of Rakahanga were evidently convinced that we were still on the verge of starvation, for they had again served up an incredible number of powerfully nourishing dishes and made sure that we did our duty by them. If half a dozen speeches in Polynesian, English and French had not give me a little breathing space, I really do not know how I should got to and through the last dish, which was a gluey, stodgy pudding.

Feeling completely done up, we tottered out into the square in front of the village hall, where all the inhabitants of the island, washed and in their Sunday clothes, were already formed up two by two in a long column. A few minutes later a party of grave-faced men appeared with Eric's coffin covered by a flag and this time the commander of *Lotus* had seen that it was the right flag. The men marched up to the head of the column, but left a carefully calculated gap so that our friends from *Lotus*, Chief Turuta and his brother, and we four survivors from *Tahiti Nui III*, could fall in behind them.

As the long procession wound slowly on over the coral reef, the depression which had tormented me for months past began at last to lift. It may have been that all my worries and all my responsibilities were now over for ever, that it was such a brilliantly fine day; anyway, I felt just as if I was recovering from a long and severe illness. I even felt physically more active than for a long time past. When the time came to say goodbye I embraced Turuta and his brother with real emotion and jumped down quickly into the waiting canoe. At the same moment some women, with tears in their eyes, struck up the melancholy *Tahiti Nui* song. It is indicative of my changed mood that this time my first thought was not of our tragic expedition but of the wonderful island below the horizon, to which I was now going home.